GOD'S DISASTER WARRIORS

Into the Danger Zone with
South Carolina's UMVIM Early Response Team

GOD'S DISASTER WARRIORS

Into the Danger Zone with
South Carolina's UMVIM Early Response Team

South Carolina United Methodist Advocate Press

Advocate Press, Columbia, South Carolina
Copyright © 2024 by South Carolina United Methodist Advocate

Scripture quotations marked (NIV) are taken from The Holy Bible, New International Version, Copyright © 1973, 1978, 1984 by the International Bible Society. THE HOLY BIBLE, NEW INTERNATIONAL VERSION®, NIV® Copyright © 1973, 1978, 1984, 2011 by Biblica, Inc.® Used by permission. All rights reserved worldwide.

All rights reserved. No part of this book may be reproduced or transmitted in any form or by any means, electronic or mechanical, including photocopying, recording or by any information storage and retrieval system, without permission in writing from the Publisher.

First published in the United States of America in 2024
by the South Carolina United Methodist Advocate Press.

Library of Congress Cataloging-in-Publication Data
God's Disaster Warriors
p. cm.

Cover photos and all interior photos courtesy of Billy Robinson

ISBN 978-1-966237-00-6

This book is dedicated to our awesome, all-powerful, gracious, righteous, faithful, loving, caring, mountain-moving, and storm-calming Lord and Savior Jesus Christ. All glory, honor, and praise to the precious, almighty name of Jesus, forever. Amen!

Introduction

What an amazing and totally awesome God we serve!

Through his son, Jesus, and the equipping of his Holy Spirit, God has performed miracle after miracle through our South Carolina United Methodist Volunteers in Mission Early Response Team. To God be all glory for the tens of thousands of wonderful, caring and loving acts of ministry he has performed through us over these past twenty years throughout the Southeast and beyond. A wonderful Christian ministry, ERT is where life-changing events are commonplace happenings, and the rewards are out of this world.

For two decades, God used saved sinners, with all our flaws and imperfections, to carry out his ministry of presence to thousands of survivors affected by disasters, including emergency responders and others in ministry. As we put our trust and faith in him, we were able to move mountains and calm raging seas. What a distinct honor and privilege it has been to serve God as his hands and feet to a world lost in sin, gloom, and destruction. Serving is not based on the worthiness of the recipients, but the heart of the servant.

Time and time again, we have heard survivors of horrible disasters tell us they were angry with God for allowing the disaster to happen to them and their loved ones. They questioned God as to why he would allow such horrible tragedies to occur. If he really was a loving and caring God, then where was he? They were filled with anger, frustration, disbelief, worry, doubt, fear, and loss of hope.

That's when they looked up and saw us and other faith-based organizations coming into the disaster areas and danger zones to help them. Their fears and doubts began to fade as they saw the cross and flame on the sides of our trailers with the words, "Christian Love in Action." Suddenly, they realized God does care, and God does love them. He loves them so much that he sent teams of pure strangers, average people with big, loving, and caring hearts, willing to endure pain and suffering alongside them plus all the hardships and inconveniences that occur in the aftermath of disasters—heat, humidity, cold, rain, toxic water, bugs, no electricity or clean water, etc.

I was in my thirties on my first overseas mission trip to Guyana in 1997 when an older and much wiser man named Karl "Blue" Miller told me, "Billy, you can't out-give God." I didn't exactly understand what that phrase meant until the end of that two-week mission into some of the worst conditions I had ever witnessed in life, including extreme poverty, heat, and unsanitary conditions. I felt so sorry for the people and wanted to help everyone beyond the church school we were helping to build. When we left that impoverished country, I and several others left everything we physically had with the people we came to serve. I came home a forever-changed man of God, having my eyes opened to so many aspects of life and and what it meant to truly live for and with God.

Many non-local missions followed—to Haiti, Mexico, Honduras, and Puerto Rico. Each time we would leave our belongings with the people we came to serve and always strived to physically give more. The more we physically gave and sacrificed, God always replenished one hundred times over. Beyond that, there was the other giving—the giving of oneself through time, caring acts, and pure love to truly show the love of Jesus in every action we performed.

The more you give of yourself to God's obedience and love, the more he gives you in return. Financial riches are a means to helping, but they are far from the riches of true love found only through Jesus Christ. I found out how poor I was and how rich in true godly living others were, even in developing countries.

In Honduras, after a hard day's work helping them trench water lines through mountainous terrain, I would muster up energy to play with the children in the village we were staying in. They especially loved my camera, and I would show them their pictures.

I distinctly remember a young boy who walked with us up a steep trail to where he would work all day in the coffee fields. As we parted, he reached into his garment and pulled out one of two mangos that he had to last him all day, and he offered it to me. I shook my head no, that I could not deprive him of such a priceless offer. Neither of us spoke each other's language, but the language of one's eyes can tell all you need to know, most times. His eyes stated, "Please take this simple yet priceless gift, as it is an honor for me to offer it to you."

I took the mango, knowing it would leave him hungry but understanding the act of pure and honest love.

Tears streamed down my face as I thought of his priceless gesture of sacrificial love. He had given half of everything he had to me. Once again, I came home a forever-changed man and even more so with each additional mission. At home we were worried about building a bigger home, new vehicles, recreational equipment, or winning a ballgame. But in the mission fields, they were focused on simply living from day to day, on survival—period. They had no further goals or vision.

That is how it is often, even here in the United States, in the aftermath of small and especially large-scale disasters. We hear, "God doesn't necessarily call the equipped, but he does equip the called." We hear the call to respond, and our hearts bleed for the survivors, and we respond with every ounce of energy we have to help them, just as God helped us through our own "disasters" in life. We feel the call and the need to help the Samaritan out of the ditch, as many of us are medical first responders but also as disaster responders. We go all-in and all-out to help while never counting the cost, for we all know "you can't out-give God."

Over these twenty years of service, the South Carolina ERT has had countless missionaries involved in countless ways with hours of service. As with any ministry, we started out small and have been blessed by God beyond all measure. As of this writing, we have ten equipped ERT trailers and hundreds of volunteers, with thousands having been trained. Most are willing to use their own personal equipment to help, such as trucks, skid steers, tractors, and backhoes.

This has been a God-inspired and blessed ministry from the beginning with all praise and glory always going to God while we graciously and humbly serve in God's mission fields of life. So many groups meet and talk about doing something, but our mission group has always put action with our words, responding to many missions each year throughout the Southeast. We have responded to all South Carolina natural disasters plus every hurricane and major tornado outbreak across the Southeast for the past two decades, putting hundreds of thousands of miles on our vehicles and countless service hours. The financial cost has been substantial, but we serve a miracle-working God who has sustained and protected us through the years.

As ERT, we are family! We are one big, bonded family of God, not just through one denomination but throughout all of Christ's church. We work side by side with Salkehatchie Summer Service volunteers, church groups, and faith-based organizations, all races and social barriers joining in sickness and good health to provide a ministry of truly caring believers.

It has been one of the highest callings and honors of my life to have led such a wonderful, caring and loving group of people. It takes thousands of people to make such a successful ministry happen, and God has provided us with awesome volunteers and leaders throughout the years, without which the ministry would not be possible.

I thank God for everyone who believed in this beautiful God-sized and God-given vision, as well as for all who dedicated so much of their lives to make it happen.

All glory to God in the highest, forever. Amen!

—Billy Robinson
South Carolina United Methodist Volunteers in Mission
Early Response Team Coordinator
October 2024

Some ERT shirts, hats, books, and manuals. All ERT members are fully trained.

Chapter 1

The Beginning
2002-2004

My first recollection of a volunteer mission was in the aftermath of Hurricane Hugo, which hit South Carolina hard in September 1989. Then, I responded with my church—North United Methodist Church, in North, South Carolina—which cleaned out our clothes closet for items to give to survivors and took them in our pickup trucks to the Red Cross.

This effort was immediately followed by my deployment as a firefighter and emergency medical technician with Savannah River Site Fire and Rescue to the devastated town of McClellanville.

My eyes were opened to the awesome devastating force of destruction that a natural disaster can produce—and the dire need to help those affected as soon as possible. They need help now, not just days and weeks later when most relief organizations respond.

At a meeting of South Carolina United Methodist Volunteers in Mission in 2002, a sign-up sheet was passed around for everyone in attendance—around 120 people—to sign up for various areas of ministry. I jumped at the opportunity to sign up for disaster response. I wrote by my name that I wanted to be a part of the newly formed disaster response mission but did not want to be the leader.

At the next monthly meeting, there was my name on the list for disaster response. I was the only one who signed up—and by my name was the title "team leader" with a question mark. Of course, I accepted the role, not wanting to let the large group of UMVIM people down, but I didn't like it. As a matter of fact, I got mad over it and gave God all sorts of excuses why I was not fit to be the

South Carolina UMVIM personnel attend a Southeastern Jurisdiction mission/disaster conference July 22, 2005, at Lake Junaluska, North Carolina.

leader: I was shy, I got extremely nervous in front of people and could hardly talk at times, and I felt unworthy and unprepared for the job. I basically ignored the fact that a host of saints had nominated me as disaster response leader, saints such as the founders of UMVIM—Dr. Mike and Mary Carolyn Watson, Rev. George and Harriet Strait, and Doris Chambers—as well as a wide variety of other foreign mission leaders such as Rev. Tony Rowell, Rev. Bruce Palmer, and Rev. Noble Miller.

I ignored the decision to be disaster response leader until late summer 2004, when four hurricanes hit Florida. These hurricanes were all headed our way but miraculously turned. When the last hurricane turned, it felt as if God had literally slapped me across my face and grabbed my attention.

"It is not about you and your abilities or lack of abilities," God himself, in no uncertain words, said to me. "It is about me and what I can do through a humble and faithful servant."

God reminded me of how Moses, David, and others had their limitations, but through their limitations, God was glorified all the more. I immediately got down on my knees and asked God for forgiveness for not believing and having faith in him as I should have.

As I started to walk in faith and trust God more, God began to open doors

Ten members of North UMC, North, gather on a fall Saturday in 2004 to place shelving and donated items on the first South Carolina UMVIM ERT Trailer. From left, standing, are Terrilynn Robinson, Laura Gleaton, Trudy Cook, Pam Mack, and Ken Midkiff. Kneeling are Billy Robinson and Patricia "Patty" Carson.

and provide just as he said he would. South Carolina UMVIM gave me a ten-foot enclosed trailer for our new team, and my home church of North UMC gave $4,000 to purchase tools. A team of ten volunteers from my local church gathered in my backyard in North in fall 2004 to put shelving in the trailer and mount the new tools.

We had no chainsaws or heavy equipment, but we were ready to roll.

January 13-16, 2005, was our first "soft start" disaster response. That's when eight UMVIM volunteers—most from North UMC—responded to Avon Park, Florida, to do a bit of disaster response work but mainly to rebuild after three hurricanes that had hit the area in 2004.

Four members of South Carolina UMVIM—Caroline Dennis, Jerry Gooden, myself, and Terrilynn Robinson—attended a disaster response training put on by the United Methodist Committee on Relief in North Carolina in late summer 2005. While at the training, a man from UMCOR was compiling information about which states had Disaster/Early Response Teams.

"Does South Carolina have enough people and equipment to compose a team?" he asked me.

I, of course, replied, "Yes"—though I really did not know how many volun-

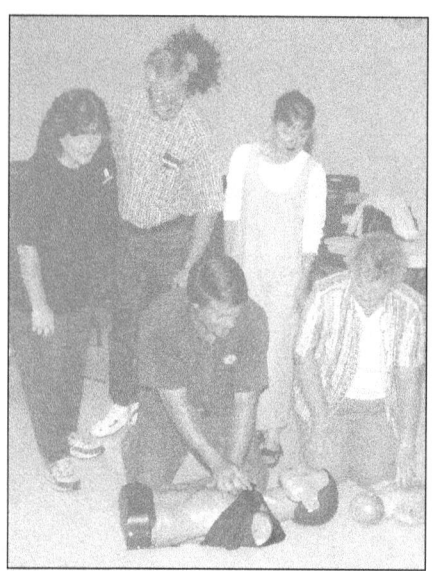 

Billy Robinson and Angela Rucker teach CPR at an UMVIM training as Angie and Bobby Oliver and Janice Collins look on.

Janice Tocar and Liama Brunner stand with the South Carolina UMVIM ERT banner they made.

teers we could come up with. After all, we four were the only ones trained.

As we headed home, we heard there was a hurricane in the Gulf of Mexico threatening the U.S. coast.

The next week, Hurricane Katrina hit the Gulf Coast with a vengeance, spreading devastation and chaos like none of us had ever seen before.

I received the call for our team to respond. I nervously put out a request and physically called a makeshift list of possible volunteers I had compiled. We needed chainsaws, slats, and more supplies. I asked for and God provided a pallet load of slats for tarps and fourteen brand-new chainsaws, along with extra parts from American Yard Products of Orangeburg and Chris Smoak, one of our volunteers.

On the morning of September 6, 2005, we headed to Meridian, Mississippi. We lacked proper protective equipment and many essential items, but equipped with faith, hope, and love, we headed out—a ragtag bunch of fourteen volunteers that none other than God himself put together to bear witness and give aid to some of the worst disaster situations any of us had ever witnessed.

God and only God made the mission a large success, taking us all the way to Gulfport, Mississippi. On a big leap of faith, we had stepped out into the historical response of a lifetime as we learned to allow God to direct our paths to devastated families and people who he had prepared in advance for us to minister to spiritually and physically.

The first stocked ERT trailer in South Carolina, above. Below, Billy Robinson shares a time with children during an UMVIM mission in Honduras in 1998.

Back home, as we returned to our regular lives, we began to realize God had worked as much on us as for the people we helped. God had changed us into more caring and compassionate people—people who would spearhead the future of South Carolina UMVIM ERT for countless disaster responses back into the

danger zones to rescue people from dangerous situations and give them restoration of hope, care, and the love of Jesus Christ as members of the family of God.
To God be all glory forever.

—*Billy Robinson*

Chapter 2

First Response—A Triple Blow
January 13-16, 2005

Eight members of South Carolina United Methodist Volunteers in Mission's Early Response Team headed to hurricane-devastated Avon Park, Florida, January 13-16, 2005. The team included Jerry Gooden of Beulah United Methodist Church, Sandy Run, and seven members of North UMC, North, including Laura Gleaton, Trudy Cook, Pam Mack, Terrilynn Robinson, Ken Midkiff, Mayor Earl Jeffcoat and Team Coordinator Billy Robinson.

The short-term mission was focused out of the First UMC in Avon Park, which itself had been hit by three hurricanes in the fall of 2004. Each of the hurricanes either blew out or severely damaged some of the sanctuary's stained-glass windows.

Hurricane Charley also severely damaged one of the sanctuary's walls and caused water damage. All of the church's damaged stained-glass windows had been boarded up but not repaired, and the damaged wall had scaffolding in place where it was slowly being worked on.

Yet this church surely had the loving spirit of God alive and well in it. First UMC had been hosting volunteer mission teams for four months while pastor Robert Thorne was coordinating teams to help the many needy families in and around Avon Park. They were putting the needs of others before their own needs, and in doing so, they transformed their church into a mission—a place where missionaries were fed, slept, and had their essential needs met, which included good fellowship and spiritual nourishment.

Mission supplies were stored there and distributed, such as truckloads of donated food, clothing, and building materials. Sunday school rooms had all been

Above, team members carry debris from a home. Above, demolition was a huge part of their work in Avon Park, Florida.

transformed into storage and sleeping quarters.

Upon our arrival, Reverend Thorne introduced us to approximately twenty other mission volunteers from Michigan, Virginia, Georgia, and various parts of Florida. Our team brought the total number of volunteers they have hosted to 224. They were really living up to the United Methodist motto of "open hearts, open minds, open doors." What a wonderful place this world would be if all Christian churches would follow their examples of expressing Christ's love

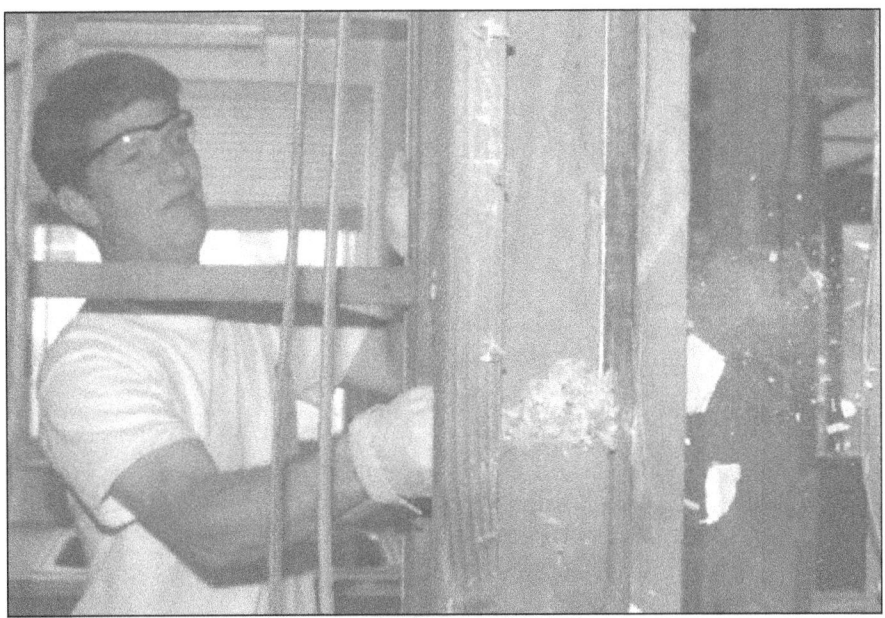

Ken Midkiff of North uses a hammer to knock down Sheetrock that had been damaged by the hurricanes.

through their actions.

Roofing was the biggest need throughout Florida, and we came prepared with roofing nails, hammers, ladders, nail aprons, kneepads, shovels, and various supplies for roofing, including a $500 donation for construction material. Because of a rainy forecast, our plans were changed from outside work to inside. But we have learned many times before to simply go where God sends us and trust him to provide all the needs and even most wants.

This led to us doing something none of us expected—demolition. Reverend Thorne laid several indoor jobs before us to choose from. One that stood out was helping a family of five whose home had received severe damage from the hurricanes, which included roof and water damage throughout the home. The children of the family have asthma, so the complete interior would have to be removed and replaced since most of it received extensive water damage. The home was valued at $57,000, and FEMA estimated the damage to it at $54,000. The homeowner's insurance would only give them $16,000 to repair the home, which included replacing the damaged roof, carpet, and some of the ceiling but not the other portions of the home that had received water damage. So the next morning we loaded up with sledgehammers, crowbars, and various tools needed to tear down walls and ceilings.

The team shows off some of their tools during a moment of fun during the disaster response.

We arrived in Florida in darkness. As we drove to our worksite in daylight, the damage left behind from three hurricanes was ever-present in the countless blue tarps on top of homes, businesses, and churches.

As we arrived at our worksite, we saw the original blue tarp material on the home had deteriorated and been replaced with a clear plastic covering. Our worksite was the home of Mr. and Mrs. Dan King, along with their three young children, just outside Avon Park. Their home was the eighty-ninth home that First UMC had taken on as a mission project.

Demolition seemed to come naturally to us, and in no time we were busy tearing out walls, ceiling, cabinets, tile, and more. The worst part seemed to be tearing out the ceiling and the insulation getting all over us. Some team members from Virginia came by to check out our progress and found it hard to believe how hard and fast we worked, especially the women, who the Virginia men didn't expect to do such hard and dirty work. But we believe in hard, dedicated work, and we believe in fun. We all took time during much-needed breaks to pick ripe oranges off the orange trees in the backyard. There was also a tree with a fruit that was a mixture between an orange and a lemon. Pam Mack of our group successfully fooled each team member into biting into a kumquat, which looks like a very small orange and has a sour and somewhat bitter taste. Later we were even able to pick some ripe pineapple at the home of the construction coordina-

The team included Jerry Gooden of Beulah United Methodist Church, Sandy Run, and seven members of North UMC, North, including Laura Gleaton, Trudy Cook, Pam Mack, Terrilynn Robinson, Ken Midkiff, Mayor Earl Jeffcoat and Team Coordinator Billy Robinson.

tor for First UMC and given a lesson on how to make the heads of them grow so we could have some South Carolina pineapple if cold weather did not kill them.

Dan King was out making a living for his family as a plumber the first day we worked, but he worked along with us on the second day and told us what they experienced through the hurricanes.

"The first hurricane blew off some shingles and flooded our home enough to wet all of the carpet," he told us. "With the second hurricane approaching, my son was worried about his treasured items getting wet, so I told him to pile them on his bed where the floodwaters would probably not reach them. As the second hurricane began to rage, we all huddled together in the middle of the house as the roof began leaking in various spots.

"Suddenly we heard a loud crash in our son's room. As I looked into his room, I could sadly see that the ceiling had caved in and fell on top of his bed, destroying all of his prized possessions. Water again soaked our home as much of the roof's shingles were blown away and damaged.

"The third hurricane basically ruined anything good that the other two had left. We have been living in a small apartment while struggling with the insurance company over the cost to repair our home. Frustrated and weary, I started trying to tackle the job on my own, knowing that we would have a lot of health problems with the children that have asthma if we left the once-wet and now molded Sheetrock, ceiling, insulation, and such in place.

"Then I heard about Reverend Thorne and how the Methodist Church was helping, so I gave him a call and listened in disbelief as he told me that volunteers would come and help free of charge."

We finished tearing out all of the ceiling, walls, and damaged interior of the home and had most of it hauled off. A new team would come in and help put a roof on and redo the interior.

Back at First UMC, we enjoyed singing gospel music, taking part in worship services, helping to cook, playing some serious yet fun card games, and enjoying various other forms of good Christian fellowship. Jerry Gooden of our team is a retired military cook. He made plans to return in March to stay a couple of weeks as a cook for all of the mission teams.

As with all previous missions, we learn so much about how God is at work all over the world, and we always receive more than we give. We received priceless gifts during our time there, such as true, loving fellowship and the distinct honor and privilege that comes through being used by Jesus Christ to help others during their times of need and spread his gospel of love.

Our team would have loved to stay for a couple of weeks and help more, but we had jobs with limited vacation time.

—Billy Robinson

Chapter 3

God's Call
September 3, 2005

On August 29, 2005, Hurricane Katrina made landfall as a Category 3 storm with 140 mile per hour winds. It devastated portions of Louisiana, Mississippi, and Alabama.

A few days later we were called to respond on our first major South Carolina United Methodist Volunteers in Mission Early Response Team response since our formation in fall 2004. I was heading up the callout and trying to form a team of volunteers to go, even though there were only four of us who had been officially trained in 2004 in North Carolina.

On Saturday, September 3, Rev. Tony Rowell called me and said he knew a man who would be a good team member named Terry Rawls in Pomaria, South

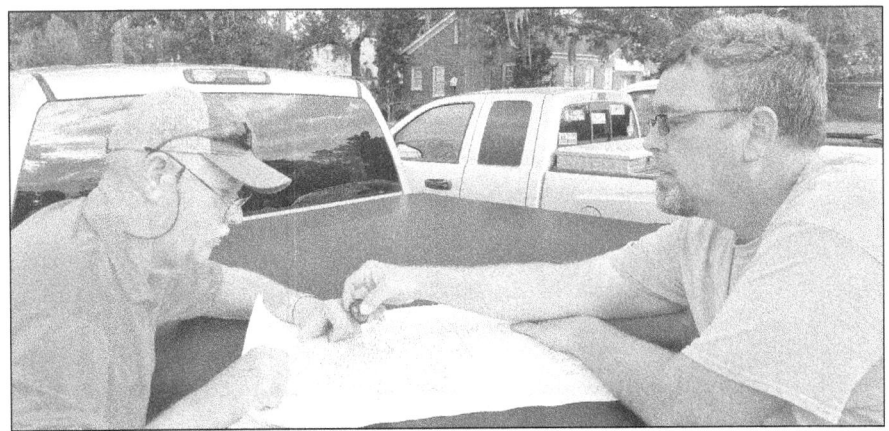

Terry Rawls (left) goes over plans with the Rev. Mike Evans.

Rawls (right) chats with a homeowner during a disaster response. Below, Rawls helped stock an ERT trailer during the early years of the ERT program.

Carolina. He gave me Terry's number, and I gave Terry a call that evening.

Of course, neither of us knew who the other was, but Terry was really interested.

Terry said he and his wife, Marilyn, had been watching the news after supper, and he'd just said to her, "Those people need a lot of help. I wish there was

Terry Rawls (left) and Billy Robinson share a smile during a mission.

something we could do!"

Just then, the phone rang—with me asking if he would like to go with our team. Coincidence, I think not. That was none other than God at work. Terry was astounded and excited. He had so much going on at work that he could not go on our first response, but he wanted to do something to help. He asked what our needs were, and I gave him a list.

On Sunday morning Terry told the story at his United Methodist Men's breakfast and asked the group to help. They donated $500. After church, Terry and Marilyn went shopping and loaded up a utility trailer with supplies such as tarps, fuel, water, food, nails, screws, etc., including supplies for the survivors. They brought the supplies, including some they personally purchased, to my home in North that Sunday afternoon and off-loaded then onto our ten-foot ERT trailer.

One day later our team headed to Mississippi fully loaded with supplies.

As we took a big leap of faith to respond to such a dangerous situation—without knowing where supplies, chainsaws, tarps, or slats would come from—God showed up in many mighty and awesome ways ... including a phone call to a perfect stranger.

—Billy Robinson

Chapter 4

Initiation into the Heat of the Disaster
September 3-11, 2005

Our South Carolina United Methodist Volunteers in Mission Early Response Team had been in formation for approximately ten months, and we had been trying to stir up interest with little success.

Then Hurricane Katrina opened everyone's eyes.

A call for our team to respond came on the evening of September 3, 2005, and respond we did. There were fourteen of us who traveled to Meridian, Mississippi, to offer our help in the first stage of recovery work from Hurricane Katrina.

With chainsaws and tarps, we began working our way south. In Bay Springs, Mississippi, we worked most of a day cutting and removing trees from a United Methodist church and covering the roof with plastic. The church had also lost its steeple. Members of the congregation were unable to attend church the previous Sunday because of the massive pile of downed trees that blocked all entrances to the rural church. The chairman of the church's board came to thank us and told about how his grandfather used to tie up his horse to a hitching post underneath some of the same massive pine trees that now lay in splinters on the ground where an obvious tornado must have touched down. Then we split our team into three groups and did tree removal and roof repair on several more homes.

On Thursday, September 7, two members had to return home, and the rest of us traveled to Wiggins, Mississippi, and stayed at the United Methodist church there, where we found we were not the only South Carolinians there to help. A group from St. Andrews Episcopal Church in Mount Pleasant, South Carolina, were also there as an Early Response Team.

In Wiggins, we found the wind damage to homes and businesses even more

The team clears away tree debris after the storm.

severe. The residents in the Wiggins area were without power, and many homes and buildings were condemned as unsafe and beyond repair. Many people were homeless and staying in local churches until suitable housing could be found. Again, we were busy with tree cutting and patching roofs with our team members split up into three groups. Several homes had been cut in half by fallen trees. The most dangerous jobs included the removal of trees from homes and covering the damaged roofs with tarps. No FEMA tarps or help was available, so we had to use plastic sheeting and tarps that we brought with us in our ERT trailer.

A huge pecan tree had crashed into the home and through the roof of one Wiggins resident, Monica Miller. The massive task of removing the tree so a proper covering could be placed on her roof to keep it from leaking seemed impossible to me, but not to the team. There was no giving up or backing down from the "impossible." After many hours and much deliberation, the awesome task was completed—but not without the help of Monica's two sons, four-year-old Hayden and two-year-old Wesley, who were constantly helping us pick up limbs.

On Saturday, we traveled to Gulfport and experienced where winds and floodwaters had swept through the area. Trinity UMC there was serving as a feeding center, food center, and center for coordinating work teams. We were sent to the home of eighty-two-year-old Sam Readman and his daughter, Pay-

Pam Fairley and a friend look over her sister's mobile home near Bond, Mississippi, that was destroyed by a tornado

ton, and assisted them in clearing out their home, cutting a large tree off their home, and placing tarps over holes in their roof. Their home had been built two feet above the required elevation for the area, yet a huge water surge had filled their home with more than seven feet of water, and nothing was salvageable on the first floor with several items destroyed on the second floor from holes in the roof from wind damage. No flood insurance made everything even more somber.

A molded high-water mark could be seen throughout the home. Water had left mold growing on most everything and had placed the refrigerator on top of the kitchen cabinets. Everything was carried to the street for future pickup by the city—all the furniture, clothing, memorabilia, appliances, everything. We removed the carpeting and the sub-flooring.

Sam's first home, in another location, had been completely destroyed by Hurricane Camille in 1969. Sam said that in a way it was better to have your home completely wiped away, as his first one was, than to have to go through all the terrible, time-consuming cleanup.

Other volunteer teams coming after us assisted with the removal of the drywall and insulation so the remaining structure could dry out before new construction could begin. We worked side by side with the family, family friends, and a group of men from Pensacola Baptist Church. Tears would constantly stream down the

Earl Jeffcoat and Sid Livingston drag a water-logged section of carpet out of a home.

The team cuts a huge pecan tree off a home in Wiggins, Mississippi.

family's faces as they searched through the years of memorabilia. Payton cried as she looked at old water-destroyed pictures of her mother and at the huge pile of destroyed family goods piled out in both the front and rear of their home, as well as hundreds of other homes throughout the area.

Sam stopped to look at waterlogged letters he had kept from his brother, who had written them as a prisoner of war during World War II. He stared at water- and mold-covered medals he had received during World War II, and then an unforgettable look came over his face as he found a small bell his wife used to ring when she needed his help before her death from cancer at age forty-six—so many years ago, yet still vivid in his mind. Sam welled up with tears as he tried to tell us thank you.

It is times like this when you realize just why we drove 1,615 miles to show the love of Jesus Christ to others during their times of dire need. So many homes were under water, and so many families were displaced with nowhere to live. We couldn't help them all.

But we at least made a difference with the twenty homes we helped and the one church building. We placed tarps on sixteen buildings and did chainsaw work for fourteen buildings and various other jobs, such as patching broken windows and even one plumbing job, all to make the homes safe, sanitary, and secure.

David Busby hammers down a tarp on a severely damaged roof in Gulfport.

Team members gather with homeowners Sam and Payton Readman. Standing from left are Darrel Briggs, Sid Livingston, and Douglas Walters. Middle kneeling from left are Payton Readman, Chris Smoak, David Busby, Rev. Noble Miller, Jerry Gooden, Bob Hunter, Danny Thompson, Sam Readman, Joe Durham, and Earl Jeffcoat. Front from left are Leslie McDonald, Sharon Hankie, Joe Finley, and Billy Robinson.

Boys watch as ERT members work on their storm-damaged home.

A wealthy woman walking by the Readman home said the storm was "a leveler" to her neighborhood.

"All folk are in the same class now—no rich or poor. Everyone's the same," she said.

At least for the time being, she was right.

Team member Rev. Noble Miller said, "I am so glad for the opportunity to have been part of an Early Response Team. I am so very proud of the Christian churches in the area—Presbyterians, Baptists, Pentecostals, Methodists, etc.—who were the first to open their doors to people who needed a dry place to stay while the emergency teams were on their way. Every community we entered and every mainline church we passed was a center providing assistance to people. Awesome!"

Every community, town, or city we encountered lost at least one person during or just after the hurricane. Each home we worked on had its own sad story to tell of the devastation from Hurricane Katrina, and some were worse than others.

But all people we encountered could find something to be thankful for. Even when they lost every material thing they possessed, they would be thankful for their lives and the lives of loved ones.

As I sat down for lunch at Trinity UMC in Gulfport, I noticed the elderly couple sitting in front of me seemed to be staring off in a daze, not saying a word

and barely eating. After a while I noticed tears in the man's eyes and that he appeared to be simply a shell of a man who was distraught, with little hope left.

For lack of words, I simply asked, "How are y'all doing?"

The woman slowly answered, "Please excuse us for not being much talkative. The floodwaters came over seven feet into our home and destroyed everything we own. We are living out of what was left of a second-story garage, and of course we had no flood insurance."

Again, for lack of better words and with tears in my eyes, I simply said, "May God bless you," as I got up to return to work with my teammates.

South Carolina ERT members for this mission were myself as team leader, Mayor of North Earl Jeffcoat, Chris Smoak of North, Sid Livingston of Pelion,

Jerry Gooden of Swansea (Sandy Run), Rev. Noble Miller of Prosperity, Danny Thompson and Joe Finley of Anderson, David Busby of West Columbia, Ted and Gloria Hitzler of Mountain Rest, Douglas Walters of Andrews, Darrel Briggs of Leesville, and Joe Durham of Pickens.

—Billy Robinson

Chapter 5

Grace Will Lead Us Home
November 2005

Thanksgiving week 2005 found a South Carolina United Methodist Volunteers in Mission Early Response Team giving aid to victims of Hurricane Katrina in Mississippi while experiencing a true, eye-opening time of thanksgiving.

From November 21-27 an eight-member team—consisting of myself as team leader, Terry and Marilyn Rawls, Jerry Gooden, Billy Ray Mathis, E.T. and Judith Smith, and Cindi Reid—responded to the cries for help.

Thanksgiving week was the first time many of our team members would be able to respond to the massive need for aid coming from the Gulf Coast after the devastating effects of Hurricanes Katrina and Rita. I led the ERT throughout Mississippi the week after Hurricane Katrina hit from Meridian to Gulfport, where we provided desperately needed emergency aid. Then and now, the Christian church represented the true compassionate, loving arms of Christ in countless missions and activities after devastating hurricanes.

The church was the first to respond and give aid well before any government agencies. The victims were quick to sing praises of the churches, which responded quickly, efficiently, and without any forms of prejudice. As soon as I returned home to a state of normalcy, I was ready to return to help more of the massive amount of others in dire need without a state of normalcy anywhere in sight.

My emotions stirred as we crossed through Alabama into Mississippi and began to see more extensive damage. We were housed at Vancleave United Methodist Church in Vancleave, Mississippi. The church was one of many churches across the 150-mile coastline of hurricane-ravaged areas housing, coordinating,

This severely damaged home in Ocean Springs was in the path of Hurricane Katrina.

and feeding work teams from various states throughout America. Most of the churches were also providing spiritual and emotional support for their communities as well as the work teams.

Vancleave UMC was coordinating work team responses from the Alabama border to just past Biloxi. The entire work zone had extensive damage, with generally the most urgent needs coming from the coastal and bayou zones. Those areas experienced massive flooding from devastating tidal surges that were twenty-two feet above sea level and even higher in some areas.

To give their cooks a desperately needed break, E.T. and Judith Smith of our team took charge of the cooking at Vancleave UMC for all the mission teams while we were there. E.T. and Tony Moore, from another South Carolina UM-VIM team staying at Vancleave, also provided inspirational musical entertainment.

We did some mucking out of homes that had been flooded. The main focus for our team was skilled labor, such as hanging Sheetrock and doing flooring and electrical work, since many buildings and homes had already been mucked out but needed skilled construction so they could once again be occupied. Billy Ray Mathis headed up the electrical side, while Terry Rawls headed up the Sheetrock and flooring.

We met many wonderful people including survivors of the devastation, church

Above, this home in Gulf Park, Mississippi, warned that "looters will be thanked" after a twenty-two-foot water surge devastated the area.

members, and various team members that had come from all over the United States to answer the cry for help. The first day we split up into several teams and joined in with other teams from Florida, Georgia, Alabama, and South Carolina to perform a variety of jobs from mucking out a water damaged home to hanging, mudding, and sanding Sheetrock in a D'Iberville home that had eight feet of water throughout. We also stabilized a roof and put flooring and insulation in an Ocean Springs home that had been completely submerged under an unbelievable twenty-two-foot tidal surge.

In the following days we continued to work on the Ocean Springs home, rewiring it and completing the flooring. We delivered Sheetrock to homes; hung, cut and mudded Sheetrock; built a pump house; wired electrical; and did some plumbing. We had a round of friendly competition with a good group of Tennessee volunteers from Franklin First UMC, near Nashville, to see who could put up the most Sheetrock in a day's time. We made friends and had wonderful Christian relationships with a number of caring people who made each one of us a richer and better person than we were before. We worked long and hard, but we had awesome fellowship and we were fed so well that none of us lost weight.

On Thanksgiving Day, Frazer UMC from Montgomery, Alabama, brought down an awesome feast that was fit for a king and his court, though most all of

Homeowners Bob and Sonja Petty gather with three teams of volunteers who helped them—one from Florida and two from South Carolina.

our meals that the Smiths prepared were at the minimum fit for a prince. Vancleave had invited some of the hurricane victims and all of the work teams for Thanksgiving dinner. All enjoyed the spectacular feast and were quick to remember what Thanksgiving was all about with a new sense of being truly thankful for everything.

The Ocean Springs/Gulf Park Community home of Bob and Sonja Petty immediately pulled at our heartstrings. Bob and Sonja are both in their mid-seventies and had just moved to the Ocean Springs area from Texas a month prior to Hurricane Katrina's landfall. They had put most of their retirement savings into buying a modular home, where they planned to live out their retirement years. They purchased the home and set it up on their Oceans Springs lot five feet above flood level—four feet above flood level was all that was required, as it was considered the hundred-year flood mark. Bob and Sonja together built a really nice front and rear deck. Then they called an insurance company to obtain an insurance policy. An insurance agent inspected their home and told them no insurance company would give them insurance without storm shutters on their home. So Bob and Sonja bought the required shutters and installed them, then called the insurance company back for a policy. To their amazement, they were told they could not be sold any insurance at that particular time since there was

In Pascagoula, Mississippi, where homes were totally washed away or reduced to piles of rubble, homeowners posted Christian signs of hope on plywood.

a named storm in the Gulf of Mexico. (In fact, all insurance companies along the Gulf Coast shut down any policy sales if a named storm is in the Gulf.)

As the storm grew into the massive hurricane named Katrina, Bob and Sonja became more worried especially as it began to strengthen and head in their direction. As landfall became imminent, they tied their boat to the foundation of its shed, closed the storm shutters, and loaded up what prized possessions they could before heading for an evacuation zone away from the monstrous storm.

They got as far away as Alabama before their vehicle broke down. Thankfully they were near a hotel that somehow by the grace of God had one vacant room left. They stayed there for five days. After getting their vehicle fixed and hearing reports that homeowners were being allowed to return, they returned.

Bob told us their story:

> As we pulled into our neighborhood, the devastation was awful. Debris and damage was so bad it was hard to get to our neighborhood. As we neared our home, we could tell that there had been a massive tidal surge. There were appliances, rubbish, and all sorts of personal possessions strung all over the place. We were so relieved when we got our first glimpses of our home. From the outside it appeared to be in good shape with only one tree through part of the midline of the roof.

The Pascagoula Lighthouse, built in 1848 out of cast iron, was picked up off its foundation and deposited intact 250-yards inland.

The closer we got to the house, though, we knew things were not going to be OK. As we opened the door, we were devastated at the site of damage. An unbelievable tidal surge of twenty-two feet had completely submerged our home. Our appliances and belongings were still inside thanks to the storm shutters, but most everything was destroyed.

Surprisingly our boat was still there, though the top of it and the shed it was under was severely damaged and its foundation barely intact. All of my neighbors' boats had washed away, and most did not even know where they were. We had no place to stay, so we went to Vancleave UMC and stayed at their shelter. Red Cross and the churches took care of us and countless others by providing food, water, shelter, clothing, and the essentials. They were wonderful—they were the ones who looked out for everyone immediately following the disaster. The churches have even provided work teams without which we would have surely lost everything.

Officials have redone the required hundred-year watermark for our area and code requirements that would make us have to place our home fourteen feet off of the ground if we rebuilt a new home on our lot. If we were able to salvage our water-damaged home, then we could leave it at its original height. The height requirement would make it impractical to rebuild.

Once again the church came through to our rescue. They tore out all of the molded and waterlogged appliances and stripped our home down to the bare studs. They helped spray bleach on everything to kill the mold and stench. They fixed the damaged roof and put in the flooring, plumbing, insulation, and wiring, including electrical panels, outlets, switches, and fans. My wife and I are simply amazed at the caring and loving examples of Jesus Christ that these volunteer mission-minded people have shown. We plan to also become Volunteers in Mission helping other people in need after we get back on our feet and things settled.

Bob and Sonja Petty purchased and have been staying in a pop-up camper on their lot so they could help with the rebuilding of their home. They stayed until Christmas, when the cold Gulf air made the camper insufficient as a shelter, and they went to stay with a son in Texas. Work teams had hung Sheetrock in their home by the time they left. They returned when new work teams arrived in the first part of 2006.

On the last day, we worked steady until 1:00 p.m. and then toured some of the massive devastation starting in Pascagoula and heading toward Biloxi. A contractor coordinating work for Vancleave UMC work teams commented, "You can drive all up and down the coast to view the damage, but once you have seen a home totally wiped out, it does not get any worse than that."

He was right. At our starting point of Pascagoula we saw such devastation that it appeared an atomic bomb had gone off along most of the coast with massive devastation spreading inland for eight to ten blocks and severe destruction continuing from there on. From there to Biloxi, it was all the same story. Many of the streets and piles of debris had not even been touched yet.

The state of Mississippi had only two remaining lighthouses—one in Biloxi and one in Pascagoula. Now they have only one. The Pascagoula Lighthouse, originally built in 1848 out of cast iron, was picked up off its foundation by the massive tidal surge and deposited intact in the marsh approximately 250 yards inland.

ERT member Billy Ray Mathis works on a roof at the Petty home near Ocean Springs, Mississippi.

Among the damaged, dead, and destroyed landscape were always glimpses of hope, such as American flags flying, neighbors and strangers lending each other a hand, and a small orange tree that had begun blooming right next to one that was totally destroyed in the Pettys' yard.

We also saw signs of encouragement and hope painted on two-ply boards and posted at two totally devastated lots in Pascagoula where the homes there had been totally demolished. One sign read, "'Twas grace that brought us safe thus far and grace will lead us home." The other read, "Do not allow Katrina to steal your joy."

The message rings loud and clear: God's grace will sustain us, and his joy will be our strength as we believe and trust in him.

—Billy Robinson

Chapter 6

First Major South Carolina Response, and Jesus Shows Up
March 15, 2008

In the late afternoon of March 15, 2008, a destructive swarm of seventeen tornadoes attacked the state of South Carolina, leaving swaths of destruction that spread across the entire state.

Around 7:15 p.m., an F3 tornado devastated the town of Branchville. I heard a cry for help from Branchville Fire Chief Alan Oakley over my Orangeburg County Fire Service radio as he described a tornado passing by their fire station in the middle of town. Several seconds later, another Branchville firefighter reported seeing the funnel cloud heading into the center of town. My wife, Terrilynn, and I were in Orangeburg visiting a friend in the hospital and going out for a meal. I told Terrilynn we needed to head home, knowing there were tornado watches and warnings all across the state. We had seen a massive storm outside our hometown of North that had produced what appeared to be a funnel cloud and turned the sky green in its center on our way to Orangeburg.

I made a call to emergency services personnel to remind them about our South Carolina United Methodist Volunteers in Mission Early Response Team, which I previously registered with them to help in the aftermath of a disaster. A familiar voice on the other end of the phone requested that we respond as quickly as possible to a massive number of trees down. At this point, thanks to interest and need because of Hurricane Katrina, our ERT now had eight fully equipped trailers across the state and 300 volunteers, about 150 of them extremely active.

Immediately, I had one of our ERT trailers picked up in North, and four of us were on the scene in Branchville two hours after the storm hit. I put out the call to action to our regional coordinators across the state shortly after arriving in

ERT members from across the state tarp a home near Allendale using heavy-duty roll tarp. In addition to the homeowners, those helping included a firefighter, Fred Tymeson, from Allendale Volunteer Fire Department; three members of Pond Branch UMC, Gilbert; Terry Rawls from Prosperity; Billy Robinson from North; and eleven from Lexington UMC, Lexington.

Branchville. Because of the many hazards present, a decision was made to stop all work around midnight and resume at 8:00 a.m.

The following morning, Palm Sunday, we had thirty ERT personnel and two ERT trailers from North and Lexington United Methodist churches on the scene in Branchville. We worked hard all day long cutting out egress routes to homes and placing tarps on damaged roofs while providing loving care and concern to the victims. The downtown portion of Branchville had been devastated, and many homes were damaged or destroyed, including the United Methodist church, which had a large portion of its steeple and roof severely damaged. We helped secure the church steeple and provide tarps for the inside.

Meanwhile, in the Prosperity/Newberry area, another ERT group from Prosperity responded after a tornado had hit its region, also destroying and damaging many homes.

A third team also went into action in the Greenwood area.

The following day found us back in Branchville, Prosperity, and into Allendale, where we learned of devastating damage from another F3 tornado. In Allendale, the major focus of damage and need was in the Concord Church Road

Members of Trinity UMC, Bamberg, apply tarps to the roof of a severely damaged home in Branchville. The team rushed to put tarps put in place before impending storms and rain the following day.

and Appleton areas near Allendale, which received extensive damage. We worked until the late afternoon, applying tarps to roofs in anticipation of a forecast of rain on Wednesday.

Because of the widespread damage, I made a request for help to ERTs in North Carolina and Georgia through the Southeastern Jurisdiction of UMVIM.

Tuesday, March 18, found us back in Branchville applying tarps to several homes in dire need after removing trees from their roofs and using chainsaws to cut out egress routes at others. My two sons, William and Jacob, and I made up one team from North. We were joined by an eleven-member team from Trinity UMC, Bamberg, and a four-man Presbyterian team from Orangeburg. An ERT group from Pond Branch UMC near Gilbert responded to Elgin and helped tarp roofs there, then headed back to a location near Batesburg-Leesville to tarp the roof of a severely damaged mobile home that took them until 10:00 p.m. to finish.

From Wednesday through Saturday, the main focus was on Allendale, with sporadic cries for help heeded in other areas of the state. Wednesday was a day of intense and aggressive action as we rapidly tried to get as many homes completed before a predicted strong storm system with torrential rains. Teams from

ERT members William and Jacob Robinson cut down tree limbs that fell on a home after tornadoes swept the state.

Bethel Park UMC in Denmark, Anderson and the Upstate, and Myrtle Beach all converged on Allendale and worked to secure tarps to severely damaged roofs until the rains started around 8:00 p.m., all while weathering forty mile per hour gusts that came with it. The wind literally tried to blow us off the roofs and made managing the twenty- by sixty-foot tarps extremely hard—it had us coming close to parasailing!

Wednesday night brought in two teams from the North Carolina regions of Greensboro/Lexington and Matthews/Charlotte. Both teams stayed overnight at Bethel Park UMC in Denmark and worked through Saturday in the Allendale area. In addition, Saturday also brought ERTs from Pond Branch, North, Lexington, and Denmark hard at work all day long cutting with chainsaws and placing tarps on roofs.

At the end of the day, we considered the "early response" phase of the disaster over, as only minor tarp jobs remained and no egress chainsaw jobs remained beyond helping people cut and remove debris from their yards. Next would be the recovery/rebuild phase, which would bring in construction work teams to help people repair and rebuild.

We had been in the early response phase for a solid week and were physically and mentally stressed out, but a lot of good had been accomplished in Jesus's

After a hard day's work, South Carolina UMVIM ERT members gather in front of an ERT Trailer at the Branchville Fire Department with the damaged Branchville UMC in the background.

name by reaching out as the hands and feet of Christ to others during their times of need. During this weeklong period, a total of 104 major acts of Christian love in action had been performed across our state by ERTs, which included: forty homes with tarps placed on roofs, many of which had their entire roofs covered; fifty-one homes having major chainsaw work performed, which included the hauling of debris to the roadside for pickup; six homes having other types of roof repair such as plyboard, tin, or shingles replaced; five homes receiving structural support to help stabilize them; and two homes having windows covered that were broken or blown out.

On Sunday evening, March 23, a team from Waynesville, North Carolina, came down and started to work Monday on the recovery/rebuild phase as a chainsaw team clearing debris from people's yards. Teams continued to help people rebuild, and churches in the region hosted the teams, welcoming them and making them feel as close to home as possible with true Christian hospitality. Homeowners continued to see Christ through the actions of these devoted volunteers. Without these volunteers, many people would not have received any aid and further asked, "Where is God when I need him?"

Jesus showed up in the forms of United Methodist, Baptist, Presbyterian, Salvation Army, other churches and volunteers, Red Cross, county and state agen-

Danny Thompson, foreground, works with other ERT members tarping a roof for a family in need.

cies, and more, all working side by side with one goal in mind—to help others in dire need. These groups worked together in one accord sharing information and resources like one big loving family, all professional, disciplined, organized, and devoted to the cause. We all learned lessons that will make future work better as we critique our responses and better perfect our disaster plans.

United Methodists were well represented across the state as people who really care and represented the UMVIM motto of "Christian love in action" in a very real and personal way. Several people commented to us, many with tears in their eyes, that they were thinking of joining The United Methodist Church after seeing our outpouring of love and care.

I thank God that he has equipped us to help others in their time of need and for the honor and privilege of being able to help in Christ's name. I truly saw Jesus in the actions of all the volunteers involved in this week's response. Being the South Carolina UMVIM disaster coordinator, I spent most of the week coordinating teams throughout the state and coordinating with other agencies such as the county and state Red Cross, Emergency Management Agency, South Carolina State Voluntary Organizations Active in Disaster, fire and rescue, local and state officials, and others. After several days of trying to do it on my own, I received help from our conference of The United Methodist Church financially as well as help with coordinating. Rev. Bruce Palmer and Lee McMillian jumped in and took a massive load off me.

The Red Cross has us on their list and they constantly called as they found damaged homes needing help across the state. We would then respond with a team as needed. In several locations, though, it was simply a case of going door to door because of the severe amount of damage.

Disasters bring out the best in people as you see people volunteering their time, talents, finances, and caring acts of love and concern to help others in need. There are always stories of someone taking advantage of others by charging outrageous prices or hurting devastated people. I pray the good in people continues to outweigh the bad and that in all of life, we will continue to allow God to use us to help others during their times of need. In doing so, we all become better people and gain true spiritual riches and fulfillment that are beyond all measure. In God's case, the more you give in his name, the more you receive—you cannot out-give God.

I thank God for allowing me to see the good side of so many people throughout this disaster. People were not worrying about what time it was, personal agendas, egos, financial cost, whether they were on the clock or not. Rather, they were focused on reaching out and helping their neighbors and fellow man. I saw people take vacation time, miss scheduled meetings and events, offer donations, cook and provide drinks for the masses, open their homes and pocketbooks, pick up chainsaws, tarps, hammers, and get dirty, all in the name of love for a people in need. I saw Branchville United Methodist Church's congregation join us in helping a community in need, though their church and some homes were severely damaged. I saw the Allendale fire chief stay in his command role, sending teams out all week long to place tarps on others' homes and do chainsaw work, while his own home needed a tarp and chainsaw work. Yet even at my requesting, he would not allow his home to be worked on until all others were done.

I am so very thankful to God for bringing us through this disaster without anyone being seriously injured, for the many work teams of all denominations, for relief agencies, for good local and state government action, and for volunteer and paid fire departments who quickly sprang into action as always. Without all of us pulling together, we would have never accomplished the daunting task at hand in such a proficient manner.

It is the churches and volunteers who really make the big difference in the aftermath of a disaster, as I've seen with all disasters that I have responded to in my twenty years of emergency service as a captain with the Savannah River Site Fire

"My joy is more than I can express," Louise Allen wrote when ERTs helped after a tornado damaged her home.

Department and twenty-one years as a volunteer assistant chief with North and Orangeburg County. If you don't believe it, simply go out and ask the victims. In Katrina and in these tornadoes, no aid to the victims was federally received, whether tarps or supplies, and by the time they got such aid, it would have been too late and other storms ruined what was left or people's basic needs would go unmet.

We must remain strong and aggressive as a Christian people of love in action in a world that largely looks at situations through selfish eyes. Getting involved in selfless acts of love and kindness is what we are called to do, making the world a much brighter and beautiful place. Please join in and help spread this flame of love throughout the world.

—Billy Robinson

Chapter 7

Lake Charles, Part 1: Major Storm Flooding Leads to Major Flooding of Volunteers
September 22-27, 2008

In September 2008, our South Carolina United Methodist Volunteers in Mission Early Response Teams were put on standby for disaster response as Hurricanes Fay, Gustav, Hanna, and Ike threatened and later made U.S. landfalls. As soon as it was safe to respond without being in the crosshairs of a hurricane, we did.

Our team arrived at Lake Charles, Louisiana, on September 22, 2008, nine days after Hurricane Ike made landfall. Ike devastated the state of Louisiana with flooding from a tidal surge that reached at least thirty miles inland. Texas had additionally been hit with strong winds. Lake Charles is located only thirty-five miles from the Texas border.

We stayed at the United Way volunteer center and arrived to a warm welcome from a people in great need of help. Though we were worn out from the 900-plus mile trip, our spirits lifted as we socialized with other volunteers from the United Way, Red Cross, AmeriCorps, and other faith-based organizations.

The volunteer center is a nice facility. It is a school that was renovated to house recovery teams in the aftermath of Hurricane Rita in 2005 and has housed more than 5,000 volunteers. They have an industrial kitchen, Internet access, dining/TV room, 200 bunk beds, and twenty showers—much better conditions than we are used to having during a response. The center and most other recovery organizations were beginning to downsize from Rita when Ike hit.

Our twelve-person team was made up of eleven United Methodist volunteers

Hurricane Ike devastated this church, as well as many others, in Louisiana. A tidal surge from the storm reached at least thirty miles inland.

from South Carolina and one of our members, Jerry Gooden, who just moved to Louisiana the weekend that Gustav hit. He received twenty-two inches of rain where he had moved but suffered no serious damage. Jerry has been with us on many past missions, and it was good to have him back as a team member again.

Besides myself as team leader and Jerry, our team included Terry Rawls of Pomaria (assistant team leader), E.T. and Judith Smith of Columbia, Rev. Ken and Dottie Phelps of Manning, Gene and Suzanne Failmezger of Summerton, Bill and Meg Roberts of Lexington, and Wayne Goff of Greenwood. E.T. and Judith were our cooks and provided a wide variety of good meals each day and even made some special local dishes such as gumbo.

We headed out early each morning to the Cameron Parish, which was devastated by Hurricane Ike, as it also was by Rita in 2005. Typically on early response calls, we are used to doing chainsaw work, placing tarps on damaged roofs, and mucking out flooded homes. But this was a totally different type of devastation. Here there was little wind damage but massive flood damage. The major damage to the southwestern portion of Louisiana was from a water surge of as high as fifteen feet that came in at high tide, flooding thousands of homes as it raced more than thirty miles inland, leaving black muck, silt, sawgrass and death in its wide path. Fish, snakes, rats, and more were found in people's yards and in their houses. Animals were dead everywhere in the flooded areas, and their stench was getting worse day by day.

We were so blessed God had given us the honor and privilege of serving him and others during their times of dire need. Our goal was to be God's hands and feet to a devastated people while showing everyone the caring love of God through our actions and compassion.

The morning of our first day found us helping to relieve the stress load of Kevin Hodge, the local United Methodist Committee on Relief representative. We helped him shuttle materials, including water and tarps, from a distribution point at Sweet Lake United Methodist Church to a centralized warehouse.

In the afternoon, we mucked out two homes in the community of Creole, which was hard hit by devastating flooding. Creole is located in the Cameron Parish, which also experienced widespread flooding. The homes we worked on not only had salt water four to five feet throughout but also black muck, silt, seaweed and grass spread throughout the homes, creating an awful stench and making cleanup very difficult.

One home was owned by Pooch and Marilyn Laundry. The other home was their next-door neighbors', where three snakes and several big rats had been killed prior to us entering. This made us very cautious while working in the deep muck and debris. Deep depression and frustration were apparent on the faces of many residents we met. They were in dire need of hope and inspiration, and through us, God gave them a bright ray of hope and the knowledge that others do care—even enough to travel nine hundred miles at their own expense to help.

Gene Failmezger, Billy Robinson, and Rev. Ken Phelps haul a refrigerator to the roadside outside a house in Hackberry, Louisiana.

Jerry Gooden and Wayne Goff put a tarp on a roof in the Cameron Parish.

The homes we worked on were ones the United Methodist church helped clean and repair after Hurricane Rita in 2005. The homeowners were grateful. They explained this was their inherited land that they love, plus they do not have the finances to relocate. Most did not have enough insurance to cover damages because of extremely high flood insurance prices after Rita. Faced with either repairing their homes or abandoning them, most had no choice but to stay. One of the homes had been through three hurricanes (Audrey in 1957, Rita in 2005, and now Ike).

Going in and out of the area, we had to go through security checkpoints, and a 6:00 p.m. curfew was in effect for the entire area.

The next day, Wednesday, we headed to an area on Highway 384 known as Big Lake, which is located on an island. One of the two bridges going to the island was damaged during Ike and unusable. The other bridge, a swing bridge, opens several times each day for barges going through on the Gulf Intercoastal Waterway. A curfew also was in effect on the island after 6:00 p.m.

During the morning, we mucked out the home of Dorothy Tolbert, a woman in her eighties who is a diabetic as well as suffers from terminal cancer. Mrs. Tolbert had a home full of antiques and sentimental memorabilia. Six inches of water had flooded the house, although her home was built several feet off the ground. We focused mainly on ripping all of the saltwater-soaked carpet out of her home and were able to save the majority of her possessions.

All throughout her yard we found washed up items—other people's docks, boats, family photographs, and countless items of memorabilia. We helped locate and salvage what items we could. The old homeplace was built in the late 1800s and had weathered at least three hurricanes. We also helped her son, Kent Tolbert, to move and locate items at his home.

Above, team members Suzanne Failmezger, Dottie Phelps, Gene Failmezger, and Jerry Gooden muck out a severely flooded home in Creole. Below, the team gathers outside Sweet Lake UMC.

In the afternoon we responded to the home of Darryl Fargue. We placed tarps on the roof of the home, which had many of its shingles blown off and even the felt paper underneath. They had no water damage from flooding, as the home had been built on blocks after Hurricane Rita completely destroyed their previous home in 2005. Our heartstrings were touched by two little girls at the home who entertained us with their tricycles and energetic play. They also made quite a fuss over the stuffed animals along with scripture gifts we gave them.

After finishing the roofing job, we had two hours before the bridge would open so we could exit the island before curfew. We asked at a fire station and distribution point if anyone nearby needed help, and they directed us to the residence of Junius Daigle, an elderly, handicapped man who had been asking for help for several days. His home had not received water damage, but his power had been off for ten days and was just recently restored. His refrigerator had not been properly cleaned out, and it had a terrible stench because of the outage. We took the entire inside of the refrigerator apart and cleaned it, leaving him with a refrigerator he could now use. This is not the typical ERT work we expect to do, but as long as we are helping others during their time of need as God directs, then we know we are being true ambassadors of Jesus Christ. To be used by God to help others in this way is not only a blessing to the people we help. A series of blessings are also bestowed upon us with true and priceless riches beyond all measure.

On Thursday, it took our team an entire day of hard labor to muck out the flooded home of Jody, Michelle, Bashby, and Bubba Thomas in Hackberry, which is located in Cameron Parish. The labor and emotionally intense job included hauling off anything salvageable to a storage area and throwing out everything else, including all appliances. The homeowners had just recently moved back in after Hurricane Rita flooded their home in 2005. All of their appliances were brand-new and now had to be thrown away after being flooded with murky salt water. The family had struggled to purchase furniture and construction materials to get back into their home and now found themselves back in the same devastating situation they were in three years ago.

They kept thanking us and even apologizing for troubling us, especially since many volunteer United Methodist teams had helped them rebuild. We did a lot of listening and counseling with them. Mucking out required us to cut out Sheetrock, paneling, and insulation in walls for several feet above the flood level. Cabinets and anything with water damage had to be torn out. The family's father-and-son team, Tony and Bubba, helped us all day. Michelle, the mother, was at work, and daughter Bashby attended school. As they entered their once-lovely home that was now completely gutted, tears began to flow. The daughter became so upset she had to leave for a while. We prayed with them and gave comfort gifts and big hugs before leaving, with them telling us "thank you" for basically ripping everything out of their home while helping to salvage the rest.

The entire town of Hackberry was flooded with at least four feet of black murky salt water with grass and such in it. This sad story is the same all along the coastal regions and bayous in many other towns or communities. One lady who lives nineteen miles from the ocean, in Holly Beach, told us she found a

three-pound catfish underneath her wood cook stove. At a Catholic church in Hackberry, at least twenty vaults and caskets popped out of the ground in their cemetery and either floated into piles or floated away. In cemeteries all throughout the flooded regions, the scenes were the same.

The mosquitoes were the worst any of us have ever seen. While outdoors you have to wear long sleeves and pants, plus cover yourself with bug spray. Inside the homes, the mosquitoes were just as bad, since all windows and doors were open.

Most of the large infestation was related to the standing floodwaters that had not receded in many locations.

On Friday, we headed back to the town of Hackberry to help Hazel Labove, who is in her eighties. We mucked out her home, which was loaded with furniture and appliances. She had also found a catfish lying in one of her flowerpots in her backyard, sixteen miles from the ocean. Again, it was a very sad situation as we removed the majority of this lady's possessions out of her home and placed them in a pile beside the road. Other people's possessions were similarly piled along the road in front of their flooded homes, as far as your eyes could see. Mrs. Labove was very good with arts and crafts and had a home full of them. The majority of them were now ruined. She told us stories about past hurricanes and how Audrey had swept her father away in 1957—his body was never recovered. Tears began to flow as she told her stories to us and began thanking us.

The majority of residents we encountered appeared to be walking around in a fog or daze. They suffered through Hurricane Rita in 2005 and rebuilt/refinished their homes, most without flood insurance. They were told Rita and Katrina were fifty- and hundred-year storms, so they rebuilt using what funds they had and through the gracious, caring, and loving help of countless volunteers over the past three years. All of the homes we worked on had either just been completed, or were nearing completion with the homeowners living on-site, when Hurricane Ike hit.

This experience left them mentally, spiritually, and physically devastated. Many tears flowed as they told their stories. You could see the signs of great loss in their eyes. Most did not know what to do; they felt it was wrong to ask volunteers to help them again though they could not afford to move as long as their homes were salvageable. They also felt the Federal Emergency Management Agency was not doing enough and they felt left out, as most of the press coverage focused on Texas, although Louisiana received the same amount of devastation.

Red Cross officials said closer to the coast, very few homes were salvable. One official stated that out of the twenty-five homes she was sent to check on, only two remained. Large portions of these regions were also still flooded.

We have learned a lot from this mission trip, which should help us better prepare South Carolina for disasters as well as our responses to disasters in other states. Our thoughts will stay with these people for a long time as well as our prayers. We pray God will fill them with hope, love, and vision as well as meet all of their needs.

—*Billy Robinson*

Chapter 8

Lake Charles, Part 2: 20/20 Vision
September 22-27, 2008

While working in Lake Charles after Hurricane Ike, several of us made a trip to Walmart after work to purchase needed items, such as rubber boots.

Unfortunately, Rev. Ken and Dottie Phelps and Suzanne Failmezger were involved in a vehicle accident. Ken suffered lacerations to his nose from his glasses and an injured left leg, but nothing serious. Suzanne suffered a sore shoulder, also not serious, and Dottie was unhurt. Thank God it was not more serious, and the occupants of the vehicle that hit them were also not injured, but the vehicle Ken was driving was totaled. Arrangements had to be made for a rental car.

Ken's glasses were broken in the wreck, so he pieced the lenses back into the frame of the glasses the best he could. His vision was somewhat blurred, but it was OK enough to work, and he finished the mission like the strong man of God he is. His tough endurance, which he had learned in the Marine Corps years prior, kicked in.

As soon as he got home, Ken made an appointment with his optometrist.

The optometrist looked at the glasses Ken had been wearing.

"No wonder you have trouble seeing correctly," he told Ken. "The lens needs to be reversed."

He reversed the lens and gave the glass back to Ken to recheck his vision.

However, Ken still was having a lot of trouble seeing clearly.

The doctor looked at Ken's eyes again. "Take your glasses completely off and try reading the eye chart."

To everyone's amazement, Ken now had 20/20 vision.

After a car accident during an ERT mission in 2008, Rev. Ken Phelps miraculously went from needing glasses to 20/20 vision. He still does not need corrective lenses today, sixteen years later.

Ken had worn eyeglasses since he was thirteen years old. Yet somehow, the lick he took across his eyes and nose in the wreck had corrected his imperfect vision to perfect 20/20 vision.

Ken still does not have to wear any form of glasses at the time of this writing in August 2024.

—*Billy Robinson*

Chapter 9

God's Perfect Timing
April 10, 2009

On Saturday, April 4, 2009, leaders of South Carolina's United Methodist Volunteers in Mission Early Response Team gathered at the home of Mike Hutchins near Lexington to stock four brand-new disaster trailers.

Since receiving a $62,000 Belin Trust Fund grant, ERT leaders had spent the last several months retrofitting and obtaining a wide variety of disaster equipment for these four trailers.

As we put the final touches on the trailers, we discussed how having the new trailers will help us be better able to respond to disasters. We also talked about the significance of getting the trailers finalized the day before Palm Sunday, the day one year ago that seventeen tornadoes struck our state, prompting ERT missions that lasted for a solid week.

At the end of the day on April 4, all four trailers were sent out to their new homes strategically located across the state to await a call for action.

Little did we know that in only one week's time, that call would come and we would end up using the large majority of tarps and supplies from all four trailers.

God's perfect timing.

On Good Friday evening, April 10, 2009, a series of seven tornadoes struck the state of South Carolina from one that hit Lake Hartwell near Anderson to an F2 tornado that hit the city of Abbeville to an F3 tornado that hit the Beech Island area of Aiken County.

A call for ERT assistance came at 11:30 a.m. April 11 from the South Caro-

Silver Bluff Fire Department had its station destroyed from the tornadoes and two fire trucks severely damaged. One of the trucks had only been in service for two weeks.

lina Emergency Management Agency. The request asked specifically for ERTs to help in Abbeville, which was in dire need of help in placing tarps on damaged roofs and doing some chainsaw work. Damage assessments were still coming in from other areas of the state.

We responded to Abbeville with two ERT groups, including two of our new ERT trailers, and helped tarp thirteen structures with the aid of various volunteer fire departments and the direction and help of Grace United Methodist Church's Rev. Eddie Taylor. Abbeville Fire Department, along with other volunteer fire departments in the area, had already done most of the chainsaw cutting.

We were moved at the large amount of storm destruction we witnessed. One man described how they knew nothing until the tornado was hitting their home.

"It was already dark outside, the wind and rain got very strong, and then the entire house started vibrating and shaking," he told us. "My wife started screaming. We headed for a nearby closet. I looked up and the roof was coming off, so instead of the closet we dove into the bathtub as the last portion of our roof was being blown away."

After the tornado, the family went outside and saw two of their neighbor's homes also had their roofs blown off and a mobile home had blown over and been destroyed.

"Thankfully, no one was injured," the man added. "We are all so blessed. Usually you simply take it all for granted until something like this happens. Miraculously, I had bought an Easter suit last week, and it was left in a closet untouched.

Above, Terry Rawls of Pomaria and Ben Pearce of North tarp a seriously damaged roof with several large holes from storm debris. Below is a destroyed Abbeville home.

I will be wearing it to Easter service at church tomorrow."

The Anderson area of the state, near Lake Hartwell, was also hit hard, including the home area of K. C. Carter, our ERT Upstate coordinator, who had several huge trees fall from his yard onto a neighbor's home. K. C. and several others ran chainsaws all day cutting out egress routes and doing some roof tarping. Another team, led Anderson District Disaster Coordinator Danny Thompson, roofed a home they had already been working on.

Aiken County officials got their damage assessments in Saturday afternoon

Abbeville Volunteer Fire Department members cut away debris as South Carolina UMVIM ERT members tarp a demolished roof.

and stated they could use teams on Sunday.

On Easter Sunday, as the saying goes, "The ox was in the ditch." That day found many ERT personnel giving up their traditional Easter services and family gatherings to aid many devastated people in need of help. They truly became God's hands and feet and reinforced the UMVIM motto, "Christian Love in Action."

In Abbeville, three ERTs put tarps on twelve structures. We worked closely with members of various fire departments and several churches, including Grace UMC, Sharon UMC, and Abbeville Baptist. The teams all worked well together in showing the love of Christ to devastated people. Our hearts were strongly moved and touched by the hurt and pain the people were expressing. Our prayers and love were left with them along with scripture booklets and care packages. Grace UMC provided us with a good evening meal.

In Anderson, two ERTs put tarps on two homes and did chainsaw work at five additional homes. K. C. Carter led a five-person team from Buncombe Street UMC and Danny Thompson led a four-person team from the Anderson District.

In the Beech Island area of Aiken County, one team from Lexington UMC put tarps on three structures and did chainsaw work at five homes. An eight-and-a-half-mile stretch of Highway 278 in Aiken County received major damage, and two deaths were blamed on the tornado. Incident command for the region was set up at the Beech Island Fire Department. We witnessed massive damage in Aiken County, including the destruction of the Silver Bluff Fire Department with two fire

trucks, one of which was brand new.

We continued our work in Aiken County Monday through Wednesday, as other areas of the state had tarps in place for impending Monday afternoon storms. Baptist, United Methodist, Mennonite, Salvation Army, Red Cross, fire department personnel and various other volunteers worked side by side in complete harmony and unison to get needed aid to people who so desperately needed it. We were able to get tarps on several additional homes before torrential rain set in on Monday.

On Tuesday and Wednesday, we focused on placing tarps on more roofs and a lot of chainsaw work. Many trees had been simply ripped to pieces, winding up on or in people's homes, vehicles, storage sheds, driveways, etc. The sheer force and power it took to break some of these massive trees like matchsticks and literally explode homes left us in awe; it was hard to conceive.

We completed nine more large chainsaw jobs and placed tarps on five more roofs by the end of the day on Wednesday. We left knowing the remaining needs would be met by other volunteers and local agencies.

Overall, ERTs placed tarps on forty roofs statewide and did twenty-nine chainsaw jobs to get trees and limbs off homes and clear access routes and roadways. We put in more than 500 hours of volunteer aid and used more than $500 in fuel, $2,000 in tarps, and $2,000 in various other supplies.

Even more importantly, we physically and spiritually touched the lives of hundreds of people all across our state who were in dire need of help along with the emergency responders and other volunteers we worked side by side with. In return, they also touched our lives and helped show us just how fragile life is. As we showed others the love of Jesus Christ by being his hands and feet, God showed us the power, love, and fulfillment that come through doing his good will. He showed us what faith, hope, and love is all about as we tried to show the same virtues to the tornado victims through our actions, scripture, hugs, prayers, and comfort.

We identified several areas in which we could better our responses, including equipment needs and our notification process. But overall, it was a very good response by all faith-based organizations we had the privilege of working together with as we strived to have a uniform and coordinated God-inspired response during this crisis.

ERT members who went above and beyond to make our God-inspired missions so successful included Terry Rawls, Mike Hutchins, Darrel Briggs, Danny Thompson, K. C. Carter, Rev. George Olive, Rev. Ken Phelps, Rev. Eddie Taylor, Frank Seeby, Barney "Buddy" Brewer, and Jason Barnes.

—*Billy Robinson*

Chapter 10

From Volunteer to Minister
April 2009

I grew up in the small rural town of Abbeville, South Carolina. At the age of fourteen, I decided to join the Long Cane Volunteer Fire Department in my community. I was too young to do all the duties of a firefighter, but I figured it was a start in helping others in my community. I wanted to learn what to do if one of my neighbors' homes caught on fire. I knew God was calling me to help my neighbors., so I got on my bicycle and I rode over to the fire department and said, "I'd like to join."

This was the beginning of a life of volunteering, because the fire department was called on any time there was fire as well as for car wrecks, storms with downed trees, and any other emergency that required a group of people to respond.

I joined Ebenezer United Methodist Church in 1999 and was encouraged by my pastor to attend Lay Servant classes to increase my knowledge of the ministries of the UMC. My pastor also asked if I had ever thought about becoming a minister, but I quickly said, "No." He also told me about the itinerancy system, which would probably uproot my family. I had not seriously thought about becoming a minister because God had called me to serve in the fire service. I always said I would get a phone call from God if he wanted me to be a preacher, and that was my way of brushing off any further consideration on becoming a minister.

On April 10, 2009, we had a large tornado come through our small town. While working with the fire department to clean up the devastated town, I met people volunteering with the South Carolina United Methodist Volunteers in Mission Early Response Team.

This was my first encounter with church folks from other parts of our state helping us in our time of need. I met Billy Robinson, Danny Thomson, Terry Rawls, and more, all helping serve God by serving others. This group—the ERT—was something I wanted in on. These people worked for three days cutting trees and tarping roofs damaged by the storm. Their help was greatly appreciated, and it inspired me.

Before they left, Billy handed me an ERT patch and one of their brochures along with some scripture. I remember saying, "Wow, they are professionally serving as God's hands and feet to everyone they meet, including total strangers."

I felt God working in my life at the time, but I could not have imagined what he had in store for me.

In May 2013, I received that phone call I so jokingly spoke of any time anyone would say I would make a good pastor. My UMC district superintendent called and asked me to serve as supply pastor of my little church because our pastor wanted to retire early.

It wasn't long before I received another call. Rev. Paul Woods, Greenwood District disaster coordinator, called to see if I would lead ERT teams because he was retiring, and I said "Sure," even though I had no idea what all it entailed.

Shortly after that, my district superintendent called and asked me to pray about taking Rev. Woods's place as district coordinator.

That year I attended my first annual conference. While there, I took the basic ERT class that Trudy Robinson and Rev. Fred Buchanan were teaching. Everything was literally running together as God had planned for me. I was finding out why I had spent all that time learning in the fire service—volunteering was God's way of training me in life to serve people. I had loved being a firefighter, and God was going to take advantage of my willing heart. I just could not have imagined he would put me right in the middle of what I already loved doing.

ERT has allowed me to serve not only people in my community, but also communities all over. The very things I was doing and had confidence in doing turned out to be his calling: serving others and preaching.

I never wanted to attend college, but I would end up having to go. I just said, "Look out, Emory, here I come." And I heard God telling me, "Be still and know that I am God."

I thought I was headed into the fire service full time, but instead I ended up serving full time. The joy God has allowed me to see on other's faces along the way I cannot describe. Just as Bishop L. Jonathan Holston has said, we are "making disciples of Jesus Christ in the transformation of the world," and I am blessed

Rev. Mike Evans coordinates emergency workers and volunteers in the aftermath of the April 10, 2009, tornado in Abbeville.

to be part of that transformation.

Today I tell people, "Listen to what God is asking you to do, and follow him. Only faith the size of a mustard seed can move mountains, and with it change the world."

—Rev. Michael E. Evans

Chapter 11

Working Side by Side and Being Good Listeners
April 25, 2010

Around 7:30 Sunday evening, April 25, an EF2 tornado swept through Darlington and devastated local homes, schools, and businesses with its 130 mile per hour winds.

On April 27, 2010, nineteen South Carolina United Methodist Volunteers in Mission Early Response Team volunteers responded to their call for help.

Volunteers came from Trinity United Methodist Church in Blythewood, Indian Field UMC in St. George, as well as Manning, Edisto Island, and various

Rev. Scott Bratton of Trinity UMC, Blythewood, listens as devastated Darlington homeowner Mary Chapman tells about her terrifying tornado experience.

Above, Rev. Ken Phelps of Manning (center) discusses work at an Allen Street home. Below, ERT members clean up debris.

other locations across South Carolina. Rev. Ken Phelps, the ERT's Pee Dee regional coordinator, headed up the response.

UMVIM's motto of "Christian Love in Action" was warmly, graciously, and lovingly displayed throughout Darlington as team members placed tarps on ten storm-damaged roofs just before a downpour of rain late Tuesday evening and also performed chainsaw work and debris removal at six homes.

The UMC motto "Open Hearts, Open Minds, and Open Doors" was also displayed as members poured out their hearts to the storm victims by listening and offering words of comfort and strenuous physical labor. United Methodists and Southern Baptists worked side by side to accomplish the majority of tarping needs and chainsaw work to cut out egress routes from peoples' homes there.

On April 28, teams from Lexington UMC in Lexington, Bethany UMC in Summerville, and from Manning returned and placed tarps on two more damaged roofs and provided chainsaw work both in the city of Darlington and the county's rural areas.

On Thursday a team from Manning headed by Phelps continued chainsaw work and debris clean-up.

Volunteers placed a total of twelve tarps on storm damaged roofs and completed ten chainsaw/debris removal missions.

—Billy Robinson

Laurie Sanders of Edisto Island tarps a severely damaged roof in Darlington.

Chapter 12

Eye Opening Death and Destruction
APRIL 21-23, 2011

On April 21-23, 2011, ten members of South Carolina United Methodist Volunteers in Mission's Early Response Team responded to a call to aid people in need after tornadoes sliced across North Carolina on April 16, 2011. The disaster killed twenty-four people and was the worst single-day outbreak of tornadoes in North Carolina history.

On Thursday, April 21, we arrived in Rowland, North Carolina, and were amazed at the amount of destruction a tornado had brought on the town. We placed a tarp on one damaged roof and performed chainsaw work at three homes, also clearing trees from roofs, driveways, and yards. We spent the night at a nearby Baptist missions camp.

On Friday and Saturday (April 22 and 23), we were directed on to Fayetteville, North Carolina. There we witnessed a massive amount of destruction from an EF3 tornado, possibly an EF4, that left one dead, several people injured, and many homes destroyed, including a minivan that wound up in the fork of a tree. On Friday it rained all day on us, but our dedicated volunteers continued to work right through the cool pouring rain being God's hands and feet to hurting and devastated people who were in dire need of love, compassion, and hope restored, along with a sense of normalcy. Friday through Saturday we placed tarps on three roofs and performed chainsaw work at seven homes.

There were a lot of amazing stories of survival told over and over by the survivors who were spared by the grace of God. For example, we heard the story of two four-by-six-foot construction company signs that were found near Raleigh, forty-nine and fifty-four miles from their original location. As well, seeing that

Casey Canoge cuts a tree off a home in Rowland, North Carolina.

minivan was an amazing sight to behold, as it rested in the fork of a huge branch that obviously had broken off from a large oak tree when the van landed in it and then on top of two other vehicles. Splinters of wood stuck through roofs and homes.

We saw an awful lot of devastation but also a wonderful amount of good through volunteers helping so many hurting people. Volunteers included Baptists, United Methodists, Presbyterians, and Mennonites, as well as people from Samaritan's Purse, the Red Cross, and various faith-based and civic organizations. It is always an uplifting feeling to see so many good-hearted people come together for a common cause when people are in need. You can see the best of people as they give their all to help others. You also see the worst of people as you witness people try to take advantage of those who are already in deep emotional distress.

Jesus was ever-present in many people and events, from us having a tire and rim on one of our disaster response trailers destroyed on Interstate 95 to a father and son going on their first out-of-state mission together. We saw various people of all walks of life working together in perfect harmony, with neighbors coming together as never before. We heard how one mother placed herself on her children to protect them from harm during the tornado.

Above, ERT members clean up debris, including downed trees, at a home in Rowland, North Carolina. Below, ERT members Jacob and Billy Robinson stand in front of a minivan that had blown on top of other cars in the storm.

We also saw God's protective hand of safety over all relief and recovery workers. We were a well-formed team with volunteer members from all across the state, including Dennis Brantley from Hollywood, Casey Canoge of Summerville,

Almost everything was blown away except the kitchen sink at this home in Fayetteville, North Carolina.

Frank Gramling and Nathan Welch of Simpsonville, Frank Seeby and Jim Caulder of Lexington, Sam and Beth Caskey of Columbia, Jacob Robinson of North, and myself as team leader.

—Billy Robinson

Chapter 13

Mind-Blowing War Zone of Death and Devastation
May 2-6, 2011

South Carolina United Methodist Volunteers in Mission's Early Response Team responded to Harvest, Alabama, May 2-6, 2011, to help in the devastating aftermath of a rash of deadly tornadoes that killed at least 337 people across seven states, including 246 in Alabama, and injured many more.

This was the worst storm/tornado outbreak to hit Alabama since 1932 and the second deadliest ever in the United States.

One of the massive tornadoes was an EF5, the largest rated on the Enhanced Fujita Scale, which carries wind speeds in excess of 200 miles per hour. Several tornadoes came near and through Harvest, including this EF5, which stayed on the ground for 132 miles from Mississippi all the way through Alabama, causing massive devastation and destroying lives all along its brutal path.

We were eyewitnesses to the devastation the tornadoes created, but we also were witnesses to the overwhelming outpouring of love and care from countless volunteers who rallied to help with recovery efforts, bringing everything from chainsaws and tarps for damaged roofs to water and baby food. Tens of thousands of people were without power for almost a week from the disaster, which decimated a one-mile-long section of the Tennessee Valley Authority's main transmission grid. That grid included three massive rows of side-by-side transmission towers that lay on the ground crumpled up like a junkyard of steel intertwined with power cables.

It felt surreal to drive through the nearby city of Huntsville, Alabama, and see the power out in the majority of the city. Businesses were shut down, and motorists became accustomed to following four-way-stop rules at every intersection

Chainsaw work was a big part of this ERT response.

since there were not enough police officers to manage each one.

Late in the day of May 2, power started being restored in Harvest, and by the next day—one week after the tornadoes—the majority of the city had power on a limited basis.

We stayed at Good Shepherd United Methodist Church in Harvest, which was also being used as a Red Cross shelter and a distribution point for food, including a food kitchen, clothing, ice, and basic community needs.

Lead pastor David Tubbs coordinated the United Methodist's regional disaster response there, setting up a command post in the rear of their sanctuary. We were impressed at the church's operation and outpouring of love from its members, plus the love shown by local and out-of-state volunteers, with people from Georgia, Virginia, Texas, besides us from South Carolina.

Volunteers all came together in one accord with the common goal of helping others in their desperate times of need. Various faith-based organizations, the Red Cross, community groups, law enforcement, the National Guard, the Federal Emergency Management Agency, and other state and local authorities worked side by side sharing equipment, personnel, and supplies. Local churches and individuals would come out to the disaster sites and invite us to eat lunch with them, or they would bring meals to us.

God's beauty could be found all around rising from the ashes and debris. We saw beauty in the countless volunteers giving their all to help complete strangers in need. We saw beauty in the neighbors helping neighbors and finally getting to know each other as they came together for community cookouts and sat outside

The Huntsville Times

MONDAY, MAY 2, 2011 » PAGE A1 » FOR BREAKING NEWS AND UPDATES, VISIT AL.COM

VOLUNTEERS OUT IN FORCE; POWER BACK ON FOR MANY

HARVEST: THOUSANDS TURNING OUT TO HELP DEVASTATED AREA **A4**

SEVERE WEATHER THREAT: STORMS EXPECTED THIS AFTERNOON **A2**

Devastation in Limestone County

Saving her granddaughter

Help comes from far and near

'We knew a lot of people up here needed help'

Madison couple join in clearing of debris at home in Harvest

By Lee Roop

Jennifer White of Madison helps Gene Fallmezger of Summerton, S.C., push a section of tree trunk into the bucket of a skid-loader Wednesday at a home on Gill Road.

ERT members tarp a roof of a severely damaged home.

on porches carrying on conservations and relationships that never would have happened without such a major power outage. We saw beauty in seeing God work through and in the lives of volunteers, making each a better person and teaching all of us to value life and the simple things we so often take for granted.

Churches were truly being "the church" as God has called us to be.

We worked placing tarps on damaged roofs and doing a lot of chainsaw and Bobcat-equipment type work from Monday through Thursday, working one day completely in the rain and two days until dark. With thirty-two volunteers from South Carolina, we were able to split into four ERT teams and cover a lot of ground using the three ERT Trailers and two Bobcats we brought with us. Each of the Bobcats was able to move large amounts of debris and equaled the power of ten men.

Most disaster sites we worked at were along the outer path of the EF5 tornado, and the people we were helping were really having a hard time dealing with all the chaos and devastation, plus the loss of lives, some of which literally happened next door or across the street from them. At least twenty-four lives were lost just around the Harvest area. There was so much devastation everywhere that after several hours you almost became blind and numb to it; it became a new sense of normalcy, as weird as that seems.

Every site of destruction is somewhat different, yet they all look the same, whether in Alabama or anywhere in the world. Two weeks prior, ten of us had been helping with disaster aid in North Carolina after their deadly tornadoes, and there were so many similarities. Eyes grow weary at the sight of so much

Most disaster sites that teams worked were along the outer path of the EF5 tornado, and the people served were having a hard time dealing with all the chaos and devastation, plus the loss of lives, some of which happened next door or across the street from them.

destruction, and our minds could not comprehend it all. Our hearts ached for the continuous pain of the survivors.

Our most visible work was the placing of tarps on damaged roofs and doing chainsaw work. But no work is more important than simply listening to the survivors tell about their terrible ordeals and offering them spiritual comfort while also trying to meet their physical needs. This can help them start back onto the path of recovery and the return to a true sense of normalcy.

Our South Carolina volunteers gave much of themselves physically, mentally, spiritually, and financially to help make our mission a success as God's hands and feet to a devastated people. But God also worked through us to make us better servants of him and to emphasize to us what really is important in life—such as me spending time and serving with my son Jacob on the mission.

ERT members responded from all over our state. From the Lowcountry were Casey and Cheryl Canonge and David Wilkins. From the Midlands were Billy and Jacob Robinson, Darrel Briggs, Sallie Clamp, Sam Caskey, William "Junior" Jackson, Laima Brunner, Barbara Hollman, and George Branham. From the Upstate were Danny Thompson, K. C. Carter, Ed Goodson, Nathan Welch, Glenn Williams, Leonard May, Jane Simms, the Revs. Donald and Karen Upson, James Morrison, Jim Lemmons, Gene Claypool, Ken Morris, and John Tomlinson. And from the Pee Dee were Rev. Ken and Dottie Phelps, Gene and Suzanne Failmezger, Ed Jackson, and Tom Sutton.

Also, on May 5, Frank Seeby of Lexington led one ERT team of seven people and one ERT trailer to Griffin, Georgia, to help with the aftermath of tornadoes that hit there. They provided aid through May 8.

—*Billy Robinson*

Chapter 14

The Hand of God Was Upon Us
May 5-7, 2011

Our South Carolina United Methodist Volunteers in Mission Early Response Team—which consisted of me, Jim Caulder, Bud Cartwright, Angie Cunningham, and Rick Cunningham—left the church around 8:00 a.m. Thursday, May 5, after Rev. Ken Owens met with us and said a prayer on our behalf. As we began to prepare for departure we noticed we might need a little air in our trailer tires. So, remembering another ERT team's experience in North Carolina, we stopped by the tire store and got about thirty pounds of air in each of the four tires. By now it was 8:30, and we were on the road.

We made it to the small community of Vaughn, Georgia, around 12:30 p.m. and met with Bill Hightower, the North Georgia UMVIM coordinator for that community. As we walked over to the site Bill wanted us to work on, he told us about the poverty of the area. It is considered one of most impoverished areas of the Griffin region. Our assignment was not the usual chainsaw and tarp jobs we have been trained to do. Instead, we were given the task of cleaning the lot of debris for the Cloud family.

The Cloud family comprised a husband, wife, daughter, son-in-law, and dog. Their home was virtually wiped out. They told us about how they'd held on to each other to avoid being swept away by the power of the storm, and how the mother and daughter had made a dash for the ditch near their home, but they said they were "placed" in the hole left by the root ball of the tree at the time the tornado passed over them. In our minds we all were thinking, "Clearly the hand of God placed them there." As I was reminded in prayer breakfast by someone,

Much of the team's work involved clearing downed trees.

Jesus went before us to prepare a place for us, and this was the "place" for these ladies at this time.

We worked with folks from Chick-Fil-A to clear the family's lot, and we got it done by the time we ended our day.

We then left to go to Griffin First United Methodist Church, where we were to stay. Once there, we knew we would not be able to clean up and rest until the church's activities were over around 9:00 p.m., so we decided to go out to eat. We proceeded to a restaurant in our work clothes, quite unclean, but still hungry. We apologized to the waitress who took our order. Toward the end of the meal, a gentleman struck up a conversation with Angie, a member of our group, about why we all had on the same shirt and what we were doing there. She gave him the details and learned he had a home in Charleston. Then the man and his family left after wishing us good luck. When it was time for us to leave, we were told that "Dr. Remington had taken care of the bill for our meal." I was a bit overwhelmed by his generosity, and I think the others were as well. We were now a beneficiary of a random act of kindness.

When we were having breakfast on Friday morning at McDonald's, a lady struck up a conversation with Angie again about our mission. When we left the restaurant, the lady was waiting for Angie. She had gone to get a thank you note for us. She had waited in the parking lot for about thirty minutes until we had finished breakfast, at which time she approached Angie, gave her a big hug, said thanks for what we were doing, and left us with beautiful card with a personal note of thanks. Once again we were touched by those around us.

The team from LexingtonUMC, Lexington, gathers for a smile onsite.

Upon arrival at Vaughn, we got a new assignment: to work on Ms. Hall's home. By now, Buddy and Caroline Brewer from Lexington had joined our team. Ms. Hall's home had been damaged a bit by the trees and limbs, but she was still able to live in it. As with the day before, we began clearing the lot for her with the help of others. A neighbor brought some huge logging equipment to help, and two men named David and Paul from Conyers, Georgia, pitched in to help. We had many trees to cut up and move, either to the curb or to the homeowner's woodpile. We also noticed the roof had a tarp on it, but that tarp was not going to keep any water out. It was being held in place by rope attached to cement blocks on the ground. We replaced the tarp and then also added a tarp to another part of the home the homeowner said was damaged and leaking. We also helped get the well repaired for Ms. Hall by assisting a gentleman who was doing this work.

On Saturday, we were assigned the house next door to Ms. Hall, which is where Ms. Washburn lived. A 90-year-young widow, until eight weeks ago Ms. Washburn was being cared for by her son. We are not sure what happened, but her son passed away, and she was now being cared for by her nephew and niece. Our job at Ms. Washburn's house was to clear the trees from her front yard and the debris from the sidewalks and driveways, plus remove trees from around the barn and debris from the back yard.

We left for home around 2:00 p.m. on Saturday totally exhausted but blessed.

So what did we learn from this? The most important fact that was reinforced is that we were there to help others by doing God's work.

Helping others does not have to be what we think needs to be done, but just what the people at the command center want us to do. We do not have to chainsaw and tarp as we expected, but we do have to touch others and leave God's message as we do.

—Frank Seeby

Chapter 15

Hope Restored
September 4-10, 2011

In the aftermath of Hurricane Irene, a team of twelve South Carolina United Methodist Volunteers in Mission Early Response Team members from across South Carolina helped in Aurora, North Carolina, Sunday, September 4, through late Thursday, September 8.

The team included Revs. Donald and Karen Upson, Frank Gramlin, Glenn Williams, Sam Caskey, Sallie Clamp, Laima Brunner, Dan Dowbridge, Monica Tilley, Kent and Betty Blocksome, and me.

We stayed at Aurora United Methodist Church, which opened their arms to us and hosted our team as well as others from North Carolina and Virginia who came to help. Stormwater had surrounded the church but had not come in. That was not the case for many others, whose homes were flooded and destroyed by Hurricane Irene.

Aurora is well known for its vast amount of fossils, many of which are discovered every year at a huge quarry run by PCS Phosphate Aurora Mine.

None of Aurora's residents could remember such a flood caused by a Category 1 hurricane. The storm dumped rain and pushed walls of water up waterways and into homes. The closest comparison was a hurricane in 1954. Though the floodwaters were the main destroyer of homes, there was also plenty of tree and wind damage. The same types of scenes can be found all the way up the Eastern Coastline from North Carolina to Canada.

Rev. Karen Upson helped North Carolina District Disaster Coordinator Cliff Harvell coordinate and organize a command structure and housing for future

Rev. Monica Tilley, Laima Brunner, and Sallie Clamp with flooded furniture they were cleaning near Aurora, North Carolina.

ERT and recovery teams, as we were the first United Methodist teams in the area. This included working on a nearby building to house teams, feed people, and set up a shower trailer.

We split into two teams and headed to various homes providing muck out operations, which included helping people salvage any good items, throw away the unsalvageable, remove and tear out all mold-forming items and appliances, then spray down the homes with a bleach solution. The main focus is always on showing a loving and caring Christian presence to the survivors, who are just starting their healing process, while also representing God's hands and feet to hurting and devastated people.

The home of Charles and Carol Stokes near Aurora was typical of many. They had two feet of water come into their home, which was enough to destroy the majority of their home and its contents, including 48 years' worth of tools that Charles had acquired. Those tools had been in two storage houses and now were strewn about for several hundred yards or more and destroyed. Charles had endured a quadruple heart bypass, cancer, and a stroke within the past five years and had forgotten to renew his flood insurance. When we first arrived, you could see the loss of hope and direction in their eyes and through their inaction. On the day we left, you could see a sense of hope and direction restored and a grateful couple who had felt the lifting love of God that carries us through such devastating times.

As with all missions, we arrived home so much more in touch with reality, blessed and thankful children of a truly loving, caring, and graceful God.

In addition to our work, Rev. Fred Buchanan of Newberry led an ERT team in Rocky Mount, North Carolina, from Tuesday, September 6, through Satur-

Above, Rev. Monica Tilley, Sallie Clamp, Sam Caskey, and Dan Dowbridge pull up flooded flooring that was starting to mold after Hurricane Irene. Below, the team gathers for a smile.

day, September 10. Teams there were also housed in churches. The main need there was chainsaw work in rural areas where many people were not able to help themselves. There was no flooding but a massive amount of downed trees.

North Carolina and all states affected by Hurricane Irene needed a lot of aid for a long time to come.

—Billy Robinson

Chapter 16

Community Unity of Love
June 5-6, 2013

On the afternoon of June 4, an EF1 tornado struck Orangeburg County. On Wednesday, June 5, 2013, South Carolina United Methodist Volunteers in Mission's Early Response Team responded with three disaster response trailers and thirteen volunteers to the Ebenezer Road area of Orangeburg County out of Bowman near the Dorchester County line.

ERT volunteers worked side by side with homeowners and community volunteers in a caring effort to help the community clear debris from homes and establish access, plus place tarps on damaged roofs to prevent further rain damage.

They also rescued a vehicle that was completely covered with a tree and various debris, as well as rescued a rabbit whose cage was crushed under debris but emerged unharmed and was handed back to a thankful family.

On June 5, a total of five homes had tarps placed on their roofs and made rainproof just before heavy downpours began. Volunteers also did major chainsaw work to gain access to three homes, and another home needed moderate chainsaw work.

We worked hard as always, but the community did also, coming together with chainsaws, heavy equipment, and helping hands to accomplish a great amount of good in a short period of time. County emergency services personnel—including fire departments and the state Department of Transportation—did an excellent job of cutting out the roadways and performing assessments. Orangeburg County Emergency Services Director Billy Staley continuously provided updated information and even took us out to help do our assessments and made provisions

Volunteers did major chainsaw work to gain access to three homes.

for us to work out of one of Bowman's fire departments on Ebenezer Road.

It was uplifting and encouraging to see people of all walks of life come together to help a community in need, including the power companies who we frequently interacted with. As always, it truly was an honor and privilege for us to be used as God's hands and feet to help others. Oh, how beautiful is the feeling of fulfillment that comes through loving your neighbors as yourself.

Team members were Mendel Infinger, Betty Wilson, Kent and Bettie Blocksome, Darrel Briggs, Frankie Whetstone, Bruce McIntire, Rev. Ken Phelps, Rev. Melvin Bell, Jerry Harris, Troy and Renee Thomas, and me.

On June 6, Billy Staley called about one more structure with a hole needing its roof secured near Bowman. Frankie Whetstone and I fixed it for a very thankful family who feared a tropical storm due to hit later that day.

In total, six roofs were secured and tarped and four homes had chainsaw work.

—*Billy Robinson*

Chapter 17

Thankfully Blessed beyond Measure
June 9, 2013

On June 5 and 6, 2013, I led disaster teams from South Carolina's United Methodist Volunteers in Mission Early Response Team to Bowman, South Carolina, in the aftermath of an F1 tornado. Little did I know that only three days later I would be in need of UMVIM ERT and UMVIM rebuild help after my home was flooded with six inches of water from a storm surge June 9 after a freak storm.

It took three months of hard work before I could move back in.

The experience was a trying, tiring, frustrating, and rough time, but it was also a time of renewed hope, much joy, happiness, and love thanks to countless hours of volunteer help and financial donations that helped offset the large cost of materials and labor I needed. The love, care, and concern shown to me by all were priceless and of such compassion and true Christian love that I will never forget it.

Because of this experience, I now have a completely new perspective and outlook on missions and heartily believe in our work with UMVIM now more than ever. I understand even more that material things are just things, but real riches are found in relationships with Jesus, family, friends, loved ones, and whoever else God places in our presence. I am forever thankful to all of South Carolina UMVIM, North United Methodist Church, North Fire Department, and precious friends and loved ones for their prayers, precious gifts of time and labor, and awesome support.

To top it off, I had just gotten married to a wonderful lady who faithfully stood by my side throughout the entire ordeal with true Christian love, care,

Bruce Robinson walks in floodwaters outside Billy Robinson's home in North. Below, North UMC proclaimed hope after the storm.

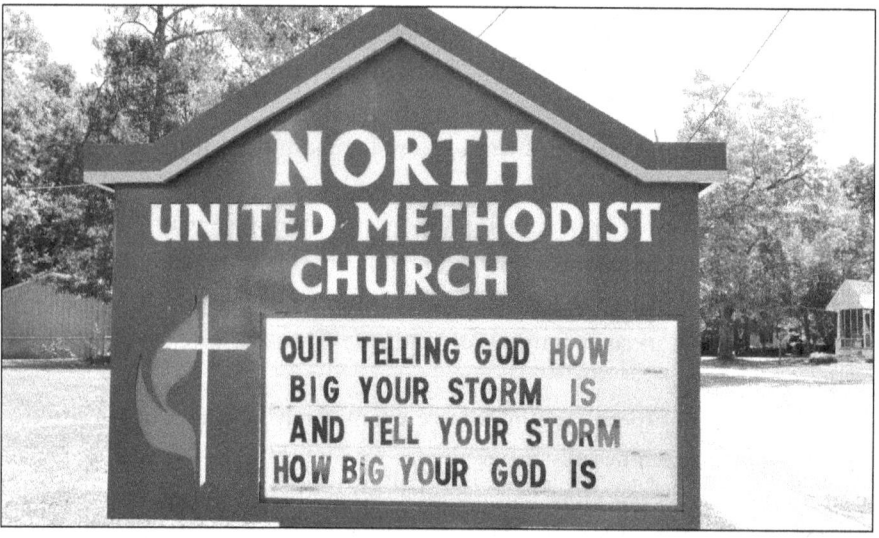

concern, and support.

God is good all the time, even when we do not understand or are able to comprehend the reasons for our trials and tribulations. When we put our faith and trust in Jesus, he will turn our disasters in life into beautiful rainbows and equip us to help others when they go through their times of need.

I am most richly blessed in the never-ending riches found in Christ Jesus.

—*Billy Robinson*

Chapter 18

Power of God
FEBRUARY 12-17, 2014

On February 12-13, 2014, South Carolina was hit with a severe winter ice storm that crippled many areas of our state with downed trees, widespread power loss, and hazardous conditions of the like that had not been seen for ten years. Some have dubbed it "the ice storm of the century" for South Carolina.

South Carolina United Methodist Volunteers in Mission Early Response Teams went into action as early as the first day of the storm helping local fire departments and emergency services personnel cut fallen trees and debris out of primary and secondary roadways.

On February 13, an ERT team located near North helped fire and rescue personnel cut a roadway out on Arnold Road so an ambulance could gain access to transport a sick child to an advanced life support facility.

On February 15, a team cut out a very large debris pile of trees and rubbish on Winslow Street in Orangeburg to free three elderly people who had been unable to get out since the storm. One was a cancer patient in need of medication. Hidden in the entangled debris was a vehicle, which was also freed.

On Sunday afternoon, February 16, a team cut access to an eighty-seven-year-old woman just off Main Street in Barnwell and found the woman had no electricity or phone and had not been able to contact the power company. Team members contacted the power company for her. Two huge limbs were also cut and removed from the roof of her house and two over her carport, plus they made walkway access.

Joined by North Volunteer Fire Department, South Carolina UMVIM ERT members assess how to cut access to Arnold Road near North for an ambulance to help a sick child.

February 17 found us back in Barnwell cutting limbs and clearing debris off the home of ninety-one-year-old Mary Hanks. We try to always leave a Christian brochure and a devotion booklet at every home we respond to. My wife, Trudy, handed a "Strength for Service" book to Mrs. Hanks before we got started with work on her home.

After clearing limbs and debris from her roof, I descended a ladder to see Mrs. Hanks get up out of her wheelchair, walk to the front door, and motion for me to come. With great sincerity she looked at me and said, "When your wife first greeted me, she asked me if I had power. I stated I do now but was without any power for four days. She handed me this 'Strength for Service' devotional booklet. As your team got to work, I opened the booklet and read the first devotion I came to."

That devotion was titled "The Power of God."

With deep emotion, Mrs. Hanks said, "Wow, the power of God! All the time I thought I was without power, I really had all the power I will ever need for I have the awesome power of God!"

Chills ran across my body as I was also hit between the eyes with the reality of

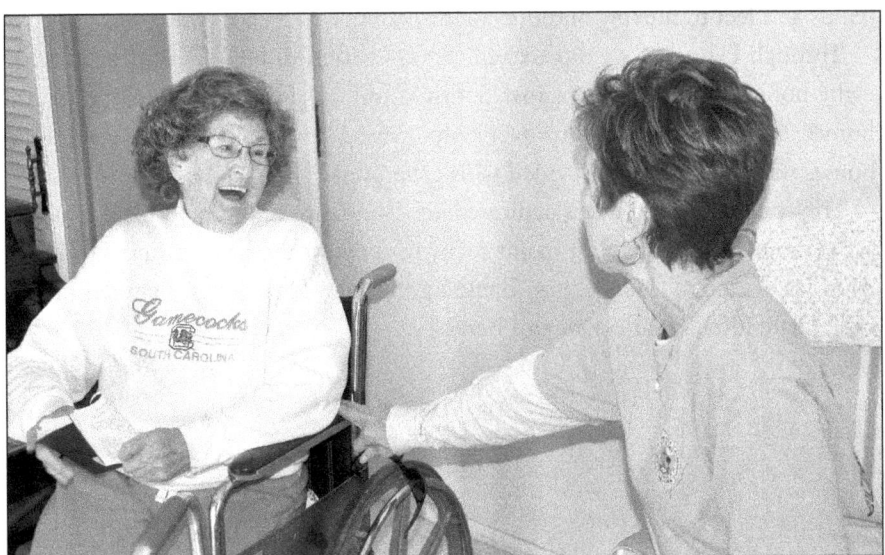

Above, Mary Hanks of Barnwell discusses a story found in Strength for Service with ERT member Trudy Robinson while crews remove limbs from her home. Below, Billy Robinson cuts a limb off a home after the ice storm.

what the real and true power of God is all about. With it we can have the courage to reach out to others during their times of need and receive priceless gifts such as the gift of wisdom from those we serve, courage to withstand all the storms of life, and faith to move mountains.

These are just four of many such situations that played out across South Carolina that we had the God-given honor and privilege of helping with as God's hands and feet to hurting and distraught people.

Through February, we did sixteen chainsaw jobs, did debris clearing at sixty-eight homes and churches across South Carolina, and did roof work at nine homes, such as placing a tarp over holes caused by fallen trees or debris. Four homes were temporarily provided with generators.

Fifty-one ERT volunteers dedicated an abundance of hours to helping others across South Carolina, with major focus in some of the hardest hit areas in the counties of Aiken, Orangeburg, Bamberg, Sumter, Dorchester, Bamberg, Barnwell, Clarendon, Charleston, and Berkeley.

—Billy Robinson

Chapter 19

Miracles Amid Grief and Disbelief
May 12-16, 2014

A twelve-person South Carolina United Methodist Volunteers in Mission Early Response Team responded to Boaz, Alabama, from May 12-16, 2014, for tornado relief aid. An EF1 and EF3 tornado wreaked havoc on the area in the early morning of April 29.

The EF3 was on the ground for nine miles and was 600 yards wide, causing massive destruction all along its path, before picking back up and then back down several times across several counties. As is with all tornados, there were several interesting stories of homes being missed while others were completely destroyed several yards away.

One of the more interesting stories was of a family of four, whose home was completely picked up with them inside and set back down structurally intact one hundred yards away next to a pond. The father went to the front door and hollered back, "Honey, all of our vehicles have been blown away." He went to a side door and said, "Honey, the garden is completely gone." As he opened the back door and saw the pond only feet away, he realized the entire home had been moved. None of the family was injured but the home was so damaged it had to be bulldozed.

People's homes were damaged or destroyed all along the paths of the tornadoes, and their clothing and other possessions were strewn for miles, deposited in trees and throughout the countryside. Many of the residents said they were considering moving since the area had experienced tornadoes in four of the past five years.

ERT members build a shed for a couple whose mobile home was blown away and had nowhere to store salvageable belongings.

As we started helping people two weeks after the tornadoes, we were still seeing many people walking around in various stages of grief and disbelief. It was an honor and privilege for us to be able to minister to them as God's hands and feet with a Christian caring presence. Our main focus in this as well as any mission is showing the loving, caring presence of Jesus to hurting people through our actions, but also through the ministry of listening with caring concern.

We were able to provide typical ERT aid by clearing debris off homes, sheds, roadways and egresses. We helped people gather and salvage belongings from underneath destroyed sheds and piles of debris, then place them under makeshift sheds and tarps. Two families we helped stated they had seen Jesus so much in our actions that they had a renewed outlook on life, humanity, and Christianity. One was planning on joining a local United Methodist church.

We also had several untypical responses, such as rescuing Daisy, a potbelly pig, from her pen that had been covered in debris for two weeks. The owners were able to feed her through the debris but could not get her out.

We were able to help one family whose home was completely blown away except for the foundation by erecting a shed to store their remaining belongings under, while also providing some shelter for them.

Rev. Fred Buchanan recalled his first sight of this family, stating, "We were running out of true ERT work in the area, so were assessing the area for anyone else in need. I drove up on the homeplace of a couple that literally had pieces of

Crews rescued Daisy, a pot-bellied pig, from underneath a huge brush pile two weeks after the tornadoes.

their home and all their possessions strewn out for a couple hundred yards across a field and woodland by a tornado. The man was standing on top of the remaining foundation looking across the field at all his scattered possessions. I grabbed my camera to capture what I knew would be a compassionate photo of grief. As I went to take the photo, I just could not mash the shutter. The hurt and pain on the man's face along with the horrible disaster scene was just too much.

"We stopped and asked if he needed help. He replied no, that another group of volunteers had helped them just after the storm and were not respectful of them or their possessions. Sadly, we left.

"At supper that night I told the sad story to our mission team. We all prayed for them as well as others. I had a restless night with little sleep. I could see the man and woman's faces and knew they desperately needed help.

"First thing the next morning, I drove back out to the remains of their home and told them how much Jesus and we loved them and wanted to help. I emphasized that we were Christians who did professional work and cared about them and their possessions.

"The couple agreed to let us help. Within an hour, our entire team was onsite and quickly got to work gathering their belongings out of the disaster zone. They had so many tools and possessions that were still good that we knew we needed to make them a shed to safely store them in. We gathered all the lumber we could, then went to town and purchased a lot of plyboard and such for the shed.

ERT members pose for a picture amid the debris.

For two days we gathered goods and built them a substantial shed.

"They were so thankful and proud of the shed and all the hard work. We left them with a shining example of just how much Jesus loved them—so much that he sent a mission team from South Carolina to help them literally get back on their feet."

St. Paul United Methodist Church in Boaz hosted our team and provided excellent meals and sleeping quarters while Snead State Community College provided us with showers. We worked closely with county emergency management, United Way, and FEMA. Our team consisted of volunteers from all across our state including myself as team leader, Assistant Leader Terry Rawls of Pomaria, Rev. Buchanan and Mike Meetze of Newberry, Sallie Clamp of Pelion, George and Rebecca Branham of Gaston, Laima Brunner of Lexington, Pete Holt of Summerville, Danny Thompson and Mark Springer of Anderson, and Gene Claypool of Townville.

The city of Boaz is named for the husband of Ruth from the Bible. It was incorporated in 1897 and it is located atop the Sand Mountain Plateau, which is labeled for its sandy soil. On the Chamber of Commerce web page is the following scripture: "Where did you glean today and where did you work? May he who took notice of you be blessed" (Ruth 2:19 NASB).

—*Billy Robinson*

Chapter 20

Johns Island Tornado
September 25-30, 2015

On Friday, September 25, 2015, at 1:00 a.m. an EF2 Tornado touched down on Johns Island, South Carolina, and caused major damage throughout a large portion of the island. Thankfully no one was injured, though there was widespread damage, including several homes that were totally destroyed.

Troy Thomas, of Bethany United Methodist Church in Summerville, is the Lowcountry Early Response Team coordinator and also a captain with Mount Pleasant Fire Department, where he first heard about the damaging tornado. Thomas led a South Carolina ERT team into the midst of the devastation Friday afternoon, and they placed tarps on the roof of Deliverance Tabernacle for Christ Church on Johns Island.

Thomas's team responded with an ERT trailer (SC-04) that had been stolen in February of that year and had all its major contents taken, including chainsaws, generators, and tools and supplies totaling close to $7,000. Supplies had been replaced through donations throughout the annual conference of UMC and a lot of help from Bethany UMC and Thomas himself.

On Wednesday, September 30, three ERT teams—from Manning, Summerville, and Orangeburg—responded to Johns Island and helped cut debris off homes and make access to people's side yards, buildings, and essential equipment, such as air conditioning units that needed repair. Four homes were helped, but most importantly, four families saw that God and our United Methodist Church cared about them as we put our faith into action.

In all responses, the first and foremost objective is to allow others to see Jesus

George Branham uses the chainsaw as team members cut and remove debris after a tornado on Johns Island.

Christ through our actions, care, and concern, prioritizing a focus on listening to people and helping them begin a grieving and healing process.

Troy Thomas said they had a great day showing Christian love in action.

Thomas added, "A big thanks goes to all our volunteers who battled high heat, humidity, and two hours of moderate rain cutting trees and piling up debris. The last stop of the day was for Ernestine Scott, a sixty-two-year-old widow. Her insurance was restrictive and would not even be a drop in the bucket for her thirteen downed trees. However, those trees were chopped up and ready for heavy equipment by the time we finished the day. She and I enjoyed a ten-minute chat on what was two oak tree stumps. I knew we had been God's hands and feet to her when she began to weep and speak of God's amazing grace."

Thomas said very often, we as ERT members leave these missions gaining much more than we can imagine.

As he said, "We leave with our muscles hurting but our hearts full of love for Jesus Christ. We will continue to proudly help fine folks like Ernestine in the coming months with this and other disastrous life-changing events."

Rev. Ken Phelps led a team from Manning to help as well. A retired United

Most of the team members gather with Johns Island resident Ernestine Scott. Standing from left are David Wilkins, Jerry Harris, George Branham, Beverly Weber, Dottie Phelps and Rev. Bob Allen. Kneeling from left are Larry Weber, Troy Thomas, Scott, Keith Rowland, Rev. Ken Phelps and Billy Robinson.

Methodist minister, Ken and his wife, Dottie, can hold their own and many times outwork most of the younger volunteers. The Phelpses have been on many ERT responses throughout the past ten years.

We broke at the end of a long, humid, and hard day with rumors of another storm on the way.

—Billy Robinson

Chapter 21

South Carolina's Thousand-Year Flood
OCTOBER 2015

On Friday morning, October 2, 2015, as rain began for what would eventually become what was known as South Carolina's Thousand-Year Flood, I was still filling sandbags and placing them at every door around my home in North, South Carolina. Only two years prior, our home flooded in what they called a "hundred-year flood" for our area. Since then, the Department of Transportation had cleaned out some main drainage pipes that were halfway filled with dirt and roots. We hoped that would help immensely, but with the dreaded forecast for unprecedented flooding all across South Carolina, I continued to sandbag my home.

As the South Carolina United Methodist Volunteers in Mission Early Response Team coordinator, I had sent out preparation warnings to all of our volunteers, all the while hoping and praying the disastrous forecast would be wrong.

As Saturday rolled into Sunday, reality set in as we began to realize the horrible forecasts were dead on.

It would indeed be a thousand-year flood.

ERT teams and individual members sprang into action starting on Monday, October 5, as the rain was still falling by helping out in their local communities. Evacuations and a massive amount of road closures, broken dams, washed out roads, and unsafe bridges hampered our responses for two weeks. But we responded in force along with many other faith-based organizations from all over the country to every accessible disaster area. Waters did not recede in some areas for three to four weeks because of the very unusual rain pattern and rising rivers that caused what seemed like biblical flooding as you neared the coast and

ERT member Misty Vazquez shares a moment with a child whose home was flooded. Often as part of disaster response, team members share prayer and other faith items with those they help.

low-lying areas. It all made the situation frustrating and hazardous for responders and homeowners.

On Saturday, October 10, another torrential rain dumped three-and-a-half inches of rain on a lot of the state, including my hometown of North. It turned already-rain-soaked ground into rivers, flooding several homes and businesses—including part of mine from which I had just taken the sandbags up. A microburst toppled over forty huge trees in North, some of which fell on homes and vehicles.

ERTs brought out chainsaws to clear egress routes and tarped damaged roofs plus preformed muck out in North as well as across the state.

Our ERTs were used to responding in small to moderate tornado events in South Carolina and were very familiar with responses to large-scale events, such as massive tornado outbreaks and hurricanes in other states. But this time, we were the victims and survivors.

We made the call early on for help from UMVIM ERTs from Georgia and North Carolina. As the knowledge of more widespread damage became apparent, our South Carolina ERT teams were growing weary after two weeks of continuous response, getting just four to six hours of sleep each night. At that point, we called out to the entire Southeast for aid.

In the third week, we started receiving teams throughout the Southeast, plus some from farther away.

Our South Carolina United Methodist Disaster Response Committee, under the direction of Gregg Varner, held daily conference calls with our district disaster coordinators, who would relay damage assessments and known areas of need. Based on this, we would send out our ERTs, plus coordinate various needs such as water, flood buckets, and health kits.

Our entire conference staff and disaster team—especially the district disaster coordinators—were vital to our response, and many took time off from jobs and family to perform their assessments, coordination, and duties. Several, such as Nathan Welch and Danny Thompson, helped coordinate in other areas since their area did not sustain much damage.

Good cooperation and communication were established from the top level with Bishop L. Jonathan Holston, then to conference and then district supervisors and finally to the local pastors.

In severe damage areas we saw good coordinated efforts among all faith-based organizations, Volunteer Organizations Active in Disaster, county and state officials, and FEMA. We worked closely with the Salvation Army, Red Cross,

Homes were severely flooded. Here, the team assesses how to offer assistance.

Southern Baptists, Mennonites, Presbyterians, Samaritan's Purse and others to share resources and a list of needs to make sure no one fell through the cracks and to ensure good cooperation, communication, coordination, and collaboration—the VOAD 4Cs.

As days turned into weeks and then into a month, we became extremely exhausted and somewhat overwhelmed. Some of our people, such as Rev. George Olive and Rev. Ken Phelps, had taken very few days off. Others—like Troy Thomas of Summerville, who is the Lowcountry ERT leader—had been in the thick of things since Day One plus continued to work their regular jobs, since ERT is all-volunteer and they have to still make a living for their families.

Our members were taking time off work to do ERT work as much as possible and using the days they worked their regular jobs as their days of rest while making phone calls to coordinate things at work. As soon as they got off work, they were right back into mucking out a home, putting a tarp on a damaged roof, or doing some other form of ERT work, including assessments on damaged homes, coordinating teams and workloads, and communicating with various organizations and agencies. Many were responding to phone calls, text messages, and emails until late-night hours, only to get up after a few hours of rest and start all over again.

Everyone began encouraging each other to take a couple of days off and look

Team members pray with homeowners at a site they helped after the flood.

out for themselves. I could easily read obvious signs of fatigue and stress on people's faces as I would visit each of the leaders in the field while bringing them supplies and talking over issues and needs. I would once again encourage them to take a day of rest, though I knew they were seasoned veterans and many, like myself, were also in the emergency services field for their careers. They knew what it was like to endure and push forth with a God-given strength and ability that's like no other.

Two biblical quotes that inspired us through this situation:
- "I pray that out of his glorious riches he may strengthen you with power through his Spirit in your inner being" (Ephesians 3:16 NIV); and
- "I can do all things through him who gives me strength" (Philippians 4:13).

After a month and a half, the majority of our requests became deferred maintenance issues, such as where an old roof that needed repair before the torrential rains was now leaking more and may also have some mold issues.

On November 21, 2015, the relief/ERT Phase of South Carolina's Thousand-Year Flood was complete. At this time, the recovery/rebuild phase began through most of the state, although there was still some ERT work performed for another month or so, and in some areas, rebuild began the week of November 9.

The ERT phase continued in the Andrews/Georgetown area through at least the first part of December with possibly some rebuild starting in areas that dried out and were ready.

United Methodist volunteers contributed more than 12,000 hours of service helping others in need.

—*Billy Robinson*

The team gathers near Orangeburg with homeowner Stephanie Givens.

Chapter 22

Peter's Salvation
November 11, 2015

In late fall 2015, we had severe floods that came into our area. Our South Carolina United Methodist Volunteers in Mission Early Response Team hit the ground running and began the long, arduous task of mucking out homes.

We were on week three of steady work, and one particular day—it was a Thursday afternoon at the end of day—we'd just finished up and were exhausted. We were just walking down this driveway, and this gentleman coming up the road shouted, "Are you Troy?"

It was kind of unnerving to me—I was tired and fatigued, and this guy looked like he was about three feet taller than me, like he could chew me up and swallow me.

My first thought was to say no, but the Lord gave me strength to answer, so I said, "Yes, sir, my name's Troy."

We met in the street facing each other, and he just kind of looked at me. I could tell something was really on his mind, really weighing on him, and he looked at me and said, "I need help."

I said, "Okay, how can I help you?"

He said his name was Peter, and we both looked at his house. It was a crawl space house, maybe twenty-four or thirty inches up from grade, and the water was just below the windowsills of his house. We'd been mucking out houses with water up to two feet, and now I'm looking at a house with maybe five feet!

He said, "I don't have anything, no insurance, I recently separated from my wife, we have a young boy, I don't have anything—I just need help."

Thomas talks with a homeowner on a call. Many times, the special moments between homeowners and volunteers remind ERT members of what their mission truly is all about: loving others in the name of Jesus.

I said, "We'll find help. We'll get you help."

The next day was Friday, and I had to be on duty at the fire department, so I sent emails out to my church asking for help. We needed manpower.

Saturday morning came, and we rendezvoused at our first house of day.

I got a call from the church saying, "We're here," and I looked out and saw a cluster of about thirty people—men and women and children. And I knew exactly what I needed to do at that moment.

I picked my phone up and called Peter.

I said, "Hey, we're going to help you today."

His voice sounded a little shaky, and he started telling me about how he used to know God but he wavered and went down a different path. But that morning, at 5:00 a.m., he told me he got up, knelt, and asked God to send help.

I told Peter, "God's sending help."

It was one of most sacred moments of my life.

He said, "Oh, my gosh, this is an answered prayer!"

The large crew of volunteers spent all day cleaning out Peter's house, using fans to dry out his baseball cards, and all day long he was saying over and over again, "Oh, my gosh, I can't believe this!"

Around 3:00 in the afternoon, Peter comes out to the street, and we're all taking a break and drinking some water, and he said, "Guys, would you mind praying for me?"

I got a lump in my throat, and one of the guys in the church group said yes, and we all held hands in the middle of the road where I'd met him two days earlier, and we prayed.

ERT is simply that—it's so much more than cutting trees with chainsaws and mucking out houses and tarping roofs. It's about being there with people in their loneliest, darkest moments.

ERT is simply Christian love in action.

That was a beautiful moment, and I'll cherish it for the rest of my life.

—*Troy Thomas*
Lowcountry Early Response Team coordinator
Bethany United Methodist Church, Summerville, South Carolina

Troy Thomas smiles during an ERT response.

Chapter 23

God's Hand of Provision
2015

In 2015, when I was surveying a lot of homes that had flood damage or leaking problems, I came across a home in a rural area near Cottageville, South Carolina. The house was very old and in poor shape. A very large tree had blown down over the house and was leaning on it, sticking way up in the air above the roof. You could not get out the back door because the tree was putting so much pressure on that wall of the house that the door was jammed shut.

The situation was above and beyond our normal South Carolina United Methodist Volunteers in Mission Early Response Team capabilities because the tree was so high above the roof and unreachable. We needed a high lift or a crane to deal with the tree.

As for the couple who lived in the home, the man was sick and permanently bedridden, and the woman was not in great health, either. They did not have money to keep the home in good repair and certainly no money to hire a company to get the tree off. They also had no insurance on the home. But they were a wonderful couple and invited me to have coffee with them and just visit. I told them that as much as we wanted to help, this tree removal was beyond our capability.

As I thought about their situation over the next few days and discussed it with our ERT leader, I wondered if we could rent a Hi-Lift jack that could reach the top of the tree and cut it down in small sections until we got it down below the roof. We had never attempted something like this, and it was beyond something we would normally do. But the couple had no way of getting any help.

We got approval to spend money to rent the lift, and I set about investigat-

ERT member Jerry Harris helps at a disaster site.

ing how to do the job. I talked to one company and discovered we could rent a thirty-five-foot jack that could be pulled behind a pickup, and if we got it on Friday afternoon and it was not rented on Saturday, we could keep it over the weekend and bring it back Monday. It was about $400 to do this, which was stretching our budget.

Someone from our church told me about another rental company that might give us a break on the cost if we explained what we were using it for. Sure enough, this other company gave us a break of about two-thirds of the cost.

I went down on Thursday afternoon to make sure the lift would hook up to my pickup truck and be towable for the forty miles we had to go. Everything worked well, and the lift was towable with my truck. In talking to the manager, he said they had a fifty-foot lift that was not rented, and I could take that instead of the thirty-five-foot one, and also that I could take it that afternoon rather than coming back Friday. This gave us an extra day to use the lift.

I made the arrangements, and we met at the church the next morning. A lady in our congregation who had worked for FEMA was at the church, and I asked her if she could go and give the couple some advice on getting help from FEMA. She agreed to go with us. She was also a Stephen Minister—a volunteer lay member trained to provide one-to-one care to those experiencing a difficult time in life—which I did not know.

When we got to the house, we made introductions. Before we started our work, we all gathered around the husband's bed for a prayer. As we began the physical work, the lady from our church was able to offer spiritual assistance as a

Stephen Minister, as well.

We could not get the lift into the backyard where the tree was on the house because it was too wet, so we had to work from the front and reach over the house. We would not have been able to do this with the original thirty-five-foot lift.

We took the tree down piece by piece and did some roof repair work as well. There was a fifteen-year-old son who had stayed home from school that day to work with us. The woman said it was a blessing for her son to see and experience that we had come to help them.

So many things happened in order for us to be able to help this family. Renting the lift was unusual, something we had never done. Then there was the lower cost of the lift, getting a taller lift and an extra day to use the lift, and finally the lady with FEMA experience who was also a Stephen Minister.

We could see and feel God's hand on this mission.

In addition, because we had the lift an extra day, we were able to get a large pine tree off of another roof, taking it off piece by piece with the lift. This pine tree had made several holes through the roof, and we were able to tarp the roof after the tree was off.

We were just finishing up with the tarp and it was getting dark when it began to rain. So we prevented a lot of damage to the second home.

Looking back, there was no way all these individual pieces could have all come together without God's assistance.

—*Jerry Harris*
Bethany United Methodist Church, Summerville, South Carolina

Chapter 24

Labor Day of Love After Hurricane Hermine
September 2, 2016

Hurricane Hermine hit Florida, then came in across South Carolina as a tropical storm on Friday, September 2, 2016, still packing wind gusts up to sixty miles per hour and heavy downpours of flooding rain. Many trees fell in the wake of the storm, and none more so than in Orangeburg County.

Fire departments and Department of Transportation personnel were so busy cutting fallen trees off roadways that a separate radio channel had to be set up in Orangeburg County designated for disaster response, which lasted well into the night.

After doing my share of cutting trees with the North Fire Department the day and night before, Saturday found my wife, Trudy, and I riding with Orangeburg County Emergency Services Director Billy Staley on a tour of damaged homes in and around the city of Orangeburg. We were doing damage assessment for the South Carolina United Methodist Volunteers in Mission Early Response Team.

We found five homes that all had huge trees on or through them. Three were too big for our volunteer teams to handle, so the homeowners would have to get a company to remove the trees with a crane.

On Monday, September 5, sixteen UMVIM ERT personnel from across the state gave up their regular Labor Day activities and dedicated it to a "Labor Day of Love." They emerged on the city and county of Orangeburg with chainsaws, ladders, roof tarping equipment, and most importantly, loving acts of compassion for devastated homeowners.

ERT members pray at a home on Mosley Street in Orangeburg.

The teams started on Mosley Street and wound up on Shillings Bridge Road, placing tarps on three homes, doing massive chainsaw work on two properties, and doing moderate chainsaw work on another. This included cutting up a huge tree that had completely crashed through a mobile home; placing a tarp over the gap to prevent further damage; cutting trees off other homes; tarping over holes in the roofs; and helping clear pathways for electrical lines.

In one home, a limb had punctured through the ceiling of a room where two people were sitting, just missing them. Several of the residents had no insurance, including a home near Cope with a huge tree hanging dangerously over it that required a crane to remove.

At another home on Mosley Street, we were able to place a tarp over its damaged structure; the owner needed a new roof and had no insurance.

UMVIM ERT members who responded were Troy Thomas, Stephen Bishop, Joe Kennedy, Richard Spencer, Felix and Misty Vazquez, Rev. Fred Buchanan, Rev. Frank Copeland, Ed Carson, Wayne Glasscock, Gary Smith, Jane Berrier, Hugh Kight, Bob and Ellie Brawn, and me. It is a great honor and privilege to

Above, crews put on a tarp a huge tree crashed through a mobile home. Below, an ERT member uses a chainsaw to cut the tree off the home.

serve in the name of Jesus to whom we give all glory, honor, and praise. The more we give, the more we receive in true riches found in Jesus Christ.

If everyone would lend a helping hand of Christian love to others and truly seek to do good, then what a wonderful world this would be.

—*Billy Robinson*

> Sept. 7, 2017 @ 2:47 AM
>
> Good morning, I don't know everybody by name, so I will call you guys the Mighty Men of Valor. I would like to show appreciation for all the hard work and dedication you guys have given to me in my time of need. It bring tears to my eyes to know that you guys exist and that I will never see you guys again. This is a new reference point in my life with God; meaning I can never say God has not visit my home because nobody but God sent you guys to my home. I thank God for each one of you, May God continue to order your steps and his Angels keep and protect yall. Keep looking down you guys are Seated in Heavenly places. Thank Yall, love Yall in Jesus name. Amen and Amen.
>
> P.S here is some Lunch Money
>
> Chris Franklin God's Favorite Child.

Chapter 25

Flood Victims Look to Bright Side of Life
September 11-15, 2016

On August 11, 2016, rain began falling across the southern portion of Louisiana. Rainfall exceeded twenty inches in multiple parishes, causing catastrophic flooding that submerged more than 100,000 homes and businesses and killed thirteen people. In portions of Baton Rouge and Lafayette, accumulations peaked at 31.39 inches, which was more than during Hurricane Katrina and Isaac.

The National Weather Service rated it a one-in-1,000-year event. Louisiana Gov. John Edwards called the disaster a "historic, unprecedented flooding event" and declared a state of emergency.

But oh, the joy that comes through serving in the name of our Lord and savior Jesus Christ. Out of a difficult situation, fourteen South Carolina United Methodist Volunteers in Mission Early Response Team members experienced the great honor and privilege through a call to serve on a mission of dire need in Baton Rouge, Louisiana, September 11-15, 2016.

It took a while for the floodwaters to subside in much of the state, just as it did in South Carolina during our big flood of 2015. First, ERT teams were called from throughout the central portion of the United States. Then the overwhelming magnitude of the disaster warranted a call to the Southeast.

Upon arrival, seasoned South Carolina ERT members received first impressions like that of previous responses in Mississippi and Louisiana for hurricanes Katrina, Rita, and Ike. The devastation seemed to go on forever in the hardest-hit areas. Most residents continuously made reference to Hurricane Katrina, with

Mucked out debris piles from homes in Baton Rouge line the streets.

several stating the flood aspect of the torrential rain was much worse.

We were housed at St. Andrews United Methodist Church in Baton Rouge, and we received job requests through their local coordinator Greg Bonner in conjunction with the UMC Disaster Command for Baton Rouge.

Our team put in three hard days working in rough situations and dealing with mold, muck out, and various forms of debris removal. We cut limbs off one home and completely gutted the water-damaged and molded contents of five homes, which included tearing out everything from the flooring, Sheetrock, insulation, cabinets, and yes—even the kitchen sinks. We then sprayed the homes down to help kill and prevent future mold. We also did mold remediation at two other homes and a wide variety of additional aid, such as helping people set up living quarters and securing their home and properties so they would be able to safely move back into a portion of their home while waiting on rebuild for the rest.

There was such a massive amount of devastated homes that it will take a long time before many will see the rebuild phase, especially since most did not have flood insurance. The large majority of people in the affected areas also lost their vehicles in the massive flood.

Physical work is one aspect of our goal, but the main portion is always centered on helping give survivors hope, inspiration, and new life in Jesus Christ through our actions and compassion. In each home, we were able to accomplish this as we worked side by side with the survivors and listened as they told their stories of survival, loss, help, and emotional depression.

One lady shared how she was told floodwaters were headed her way, but she chose not to believe it as it had never happened in her thirty-plus years in her home. Her mind was changed as she saw the waters come up her street so quickly that, as she tried to escape, the ever-rising water flooded out her car and she was forced to retreat into her home with her pet dachshund. A neighbor later rescued them in her boat. To do so, they had to break down a portion of her wooden fence.

After completing her home, we also replaced the broken fence so she could bring her pet home with her into a secured yard and second-story room that we helped set up for her to stay in.

Everywhere we went, we heard survivor stories and how people were grateful though their homes were devastated and most of their possessions destroyed.

Team members remove damaged flooring.

Some were depressed and desperate for help, but most were still holding out hope. They were encouraging to us.

The people there will need help and a lot of it for a long period of time. There is a lack of volunteers to help and the need is dire, especially since the large majority had no flood insurance, as many did not live in what was considered a flood plain.

South Carolina ERT members who responded to Baton Rouge were myself as team leader with my wife, Trudy, Assistant Leader Chuck Marshall of Chesnee, Jill Evans (our chef) of Salem, Pat Coleman and Cherlynn Hewitt of Boiling Springs, Robert "Bob" Nichols of Campobello, Ed Rothe of Hartsville, Keith Rowland and Joe Kennedy of Summerville, Richard Spencer of Ladson, Hugh Kight of Charleston, George Branham of Gaston, and Laima Brunner of Lexington.

—*Billy Robinson*

Chapter 26

Devastating Damage, Miraculous Saves
October 8-15, 2016

Hurricane Matthew hit South Carolina on October 8. The following morning, our United Methodist Early Response Teams headed into disaster zones to help our brothers and sisters whose homes and lives had been devastated by massive winds that had toppled trees onto and into their homes.

Over the period of a week, ERT teams across our state worked on sixty-five homes, removing trees, placing tarps on homes, and mucking out flooded homes.

Following are two of the many survivor stories.

The day Hurricane Matthew slammed into South Carolina, many emergency responders across our state started responding to emergencies as soon as the winds died down enough that it was safe to do so. My wife, Trudy, and I responded with our volunteer fire department in North to various calls, including many trees down across roadways.

In the midst of it, I received a text from Orangeburg County Emergency Services stating, "Urgent, give the Emergency Operations Center a call." I learned a major wind event from the backside of the storm had devastated parts of Orangeburg. We performed damage assessments and rallied an ERT response for the following morning.

We started at the home of Richie and Lisa Hall on Perryclear Road. Tears filled Lisa's eyes as we made our way through the maze of fallen power lines and trees to their home. More tears flowed as she told how her family had literally run for their lives during the storm that had severely damaged their home. Three

At one home, trees were strewn throughout the yard and onto a neighbor's home.

huge pines were on their home, with several limbs penetrating into their living quarters. Trees were also strewn throughout their yard and onto their neighbor's home.

We quickly went to work clearing the debris. As the day wore on, neighbors began coming over to help drag limbs and even assist us with putting a tarp over nine holes in the Halls' roof. It became a wonderful, loving, and caring community response that once again brought tears to Lisa's eyes.

Tears continued as Lisa's small son asked that we all gather together for a prayer at the end of the strenuous ordeal that had the family back safely into their home, though they would go several more days without power.

The following day found us at the home of seventy-seven-year-old John Fair, on High Street in Orangeburg. When one of our damage assessment teams—comprising Laima Brunner and Janice Tocar—arrived on Monday morning, John started praising Jesus. He praised our Lord more when our ERT crew arrived that afternoon.

Above, massive winds toppled trees onto and into homes. Below left, a downed power line. Below right, ERTs chat with homeowners.

Half of his home was covered with a huge pecan tree. John called our team inside to his bedroom stating he needed to tell us how good God had been to him.

As he told us, "I was lying in my bed when all of a sudden I heard a large crash. I looked up to see a big limb with a pointed fork on it coming through the roof and ceiling straight at me. I thought I was dead. Then miraculously, the limb broke off and floated down, coming to rest beside me on the bed. Insulation and rain water started falling on me. I was stunned. I knew that my home was damaged, but I also knew that my life had miraculously been spared. And then your disaster response team arrived in the form of another miracle, as we had no one

The team gathers for a smile with the homeowner.

to help us. I just have to praise the Lord!"

We cut the limbs away from his home and applied a tarp over the damaged roof. We went away with a new friend, humbly blessed through a man named John who praised the name of Jesus.

—Billy Robinson

Chapter 27

Fred Buchanan to the Rescue
FALL 2016

In the fall of 2016, Disaster Recovery Ministries in the South Carolina Conference of The United Methodist Church was asked to help a family with a large tree that was leaning over and partially resting on the metal roof of their home.

Ward Smith, author of this story, works on a roof.

Rev. Fred Buchanan with his invention, the Fred Device.

I called South Carolina United Methodist Volunteers in Mission Early Response Team instructor and team leader Rev. Fred Buchanan because I needed the ERT experience and know-how of someone who could figure out the best way to safely remove this massive tree.

When we arrived, Fred assessed the situation and asked me to help him on the peak of the steep roof. I was willing to help but not sure how to get up to the peak and move around.

Fred went to the ERT trailer and found hinged 1- by 6-inch pieces of wood with short 2- by 4-inch pieces attached like a ladder. As I perched on the peak of the roof, Fred carefully cut the seemly endless number of limbs until the top of the tree was off the roof and we could tarp the hole.

I am so thankful for Rev. Fred Buchanan and his dedication and willingness to work and give completely to help families in need.

—*Ward Smith*

Chapter 28

Q&A with the Leader of South Carolina's ERT
November 10, 2016

As a way to help supporters of United Methodist Volunteers in Mission understand the hard work put in by those who consistently serve through UMVIM's various ministry efforts, UMVIM interviewed South Carolina's Early Response Team Coordinator Billy Robinson on his experience with the disaster response ministry.

Q: How do volunteers help you carry out your mission as the coordinator of Early Response Teams in South Carolina?

A: We in South Carolina, like most everywhere, are all volunteers. Without volunteers we would have no Early Response Teams, and we would miss out on so many dire needs and opportunities to allow God's love to flow through us in our actions, care, love, and concern for others. Coordinating disaster response is chaotic, especially in the early stages of any disaster, such as our October 2015 floods and recent Tropical Storm Hermine. It is the same in emergency response, like my paid profession as a fire officer/paramedic. It is vital to have people who will fill in leadership positions and coordinate responses in regional locations, especially in large scale disasters. Without them and all the other wonderful volunteers and support across UMVIM and The United Methodist Church, it would be impossible.

Volunteers are the backbone of all we do: helping with training (we have eight UMCOR trainers); preparing and maintaining our seven ERT trailers; providing leadership as team leaders and regional coordinators; and participating on our state ERT board. Of course, volunteers are the hard-working, dedicated people who put tarps on roofs, run chainsaws, and muck out while always being listeners across South Carolina, the Southeast, and the entire United States. A South Carolina ERT team recently came back from Louisiana.

Q: What differences do you see in teams whose leaders have been trained by UMVIM-SEJ?

A: We require our leaders to be trained through UMVIM and ERT. This gives them a firm foundation of expectations and quality management that we expect out of them and their teams. It instills in them the true Christian values and attitudes that we expect them and their team members to put forth at all times.

Q: Can you share a brief story about the impact of volunteers?

A: During our South Carolina "One in 1,000-Year Flood" of October 2015, we quickly became overwhelmed, especially across the Midlands to the coast. One of the hardest-hit areas was the Charleston/Summerville area. I immediately called out to Troy Thomas, who is our Lowcountry ERT coordinator (our state is divided in four regions, and we have an ERT coordinator and two assistants in each). He already had volunteers out helping people on Day One and continued coordinating ERT efforts for three months among various agencies and organizations, plus teams coming in to South Carolina from other states. His wife, Renee, was instrumental in helping get teams housed and taken care of. Troy also performed his paid job as an officer with Mount Pleasant Fire Department on the days he was not doing muck outs, and he let his secondary construction business lapse for the three-month period.

Many times we do not see the impact or fruits of our labor, but Troy saw it firsthand in a man named Peter. Peter was a big man who was angered that his home was flooded and no one had made it out to help him. He also had very little to do with the church or Christians. He flagged Troy down in the street and told him that he needed help. Troy turned to see Peter's flooded home with water still up to the windows. As soon as the floodwaters subsided, Troy was able to send a team of thirty-two people in to help Peter. Peter began to see the love, care, and compassion of Jesus Christ through the ERT volunteers' witness of Christian love in action, including their intensive labor to muck out his home. At the end of the day, they all gathered together in a circle in the street in front of Peter's home to pray. During the prayer, Peter broke down to his knees and, with the ERT gathered around him, he gave his life to Jesus Christ!

We even saw volunteers cross state, district, and conference lines to help. In the Pee Dee Region (Georgetown to Myrtle Beach) of our state, the ERT coordinator, Rev. Ken Phelps, was land-locked for three days because of roadways and bridges being washed out. So, Rev. George Olive of Surfside Beach helped coordinate ERT efforts and provide assessments along with Ann Huffman and others from North Carolina ERT until Ken could get freed.

They continued to assist Ken for months because of the widespread damage.

—Courtesy of UMVIM-SEJ

Chapter 29

Nichols Work Blitz Exemplifies Love in Action
December 2-3, 2016

Hurricane Matthew swamped the Nichols and Mullins area of South Carolina, flooding all the churches, nearly all the businesses, and more than 230 homes. Many families lost almost everything they owned.

But thanks to the efforts of 236 United Methodist volunteers from across the state, many of them members of the South Carolina United Methodist Volunteers in Mission Early Response Team, they have new hope and a strong sense of Christian love and support.

ERT members teamed up with South Carolina Conference disaster response for a work blitz in Nichols and Mullins December 2-3, 2016, doing tear-out and mold remediation for eighteen flooded homes in preparation for the next step, long-term recovery and rebuild.

Armed with hammers, masks and other supplies, teams spent two days removing drywall, pulling out flooring, carting out debris, spraying for mold and more. The work blitz was the first of its kind, and the results exceeded organizers' expectations and brought both victims and volunteers to their knees in gratitude.

"It was phenomenal," said Matt Brodie, then-conference disaster response coordinator and ERT member, who came up with the idea for the blitz as a way for the UMC to be the hands and feet of Christ after the hurricane.

Organizers, including disaster response coordinators from every district in South Carolina, had hoped to get one hundred people to help. Getting 236 from all over the state, as well as a few from Georgia, North Carolina, Minnesota and Texas, was "really inspiring," Brodie said.

Above, volunteers pray before helping clean up the devastation in Nichols and Mullins. Below left, protective equipment kept volunteers safe from mold an other toxins. Below right, a volunteer sprays a home for mold.

"The amount of resources and people that we brought to Nichols made a huge impact on that community," Brodie said. "Beyond doing the tear-out and helping people physically with their homes, we wanted to provide hope and a sense that they are not forgotten and that there are people who are there for them and want to help, and I think we provided that on a scale much bigger than I had ever imagined."

At a luncheon the first day of the blitz, South Carolina Resident Bishop Jonathan Holston praised the crowd of volunteers for stepping up to help.

"You are doing what we all ought to do: to live our faith ... and to put words into action," Holston said, noting the church's message of transformation is going out into the countryside with joy. "Whenever we gather—whether with a hammer or a Bible, whether with a shovel or a hymnal—it should be a spiritual revival."

Nichols Mayor Lawson Battle, who himself lost everything in the flood, said it will take a miracle to fix Nichols, and he knows the miracle is happening before his eyes as he watches people come to the community in Christian service.

"Y'all are the ones giving the citizens hope to go forward," Battle told the crowd of volunteers at the luncheon. "Y'all are wonderful and are doing such a great thing."

"It was truly a wonderful expression of United Methodist Christian love in action," said Billy Robinson, coordinator of South Carolina UMVIM ERT.

—*Jessica Brodie, editor*
South Carolina United Methodist Advocate

Chapter 30

'A Total Faith Lift'
January 13-14, 2017

On the heels of a wildly successful work blitz in Nichols, South Carolina, more than 150 volunteers—many of them South Carolina United Methodist Volunteers in Mission Early Response Team members—headed to Sellers January 13-14, 2017, ready to help in the aftermath of some of the worst flooding this state has experienced.

"It was just a total faith lift, a joy to know that someone thought enough to come and help us," said homeowner Allen James, whose Sellers home was devastated both by October's Hurricane Matthew and the October 2015 flood.

Sellers, already a poverty-stricken area before the hurricane, was badly impacted after two storm-swamped rivers overflowed and flooded the region. Nearly everyone in the town suffered damage. But after the January 13-14 hurricane blitz organized by the South Carolina Conference of The United Methodist Church, with heavy involvement by the South Carolina UMVIM ERT, many of those homeowners were on the road to recovery.

"You can see the smiles on everybody's faces," James said, his eyes shining with tears as he watched teams of volunteers work on his home and up and down his street. He said the commitment of the volunteers warmed his heart. "It wasn't 'we're going to help' and we don't see them anymore. They said they were going to help, and they're here. They're doing this and this, and they're helping next door and down the street, and it gives you a feeling like—wow. It's just wonderful."

James's modest one-story home on Bank Street was one of two dozen homes helped by United Methodist volunteers that weekend.

ERT members and other volunteers work on a damaged roof in Sellers.

Volunteers did everything from mold removal and tearout of drywall and flooring to roof repairs, cabinetry, and bathroom rebuilds.

"We've set some pretty substantial precedents about how we respond to disaster," said Matt Brodie, then conference disaster response coordinator, calling the volunteers the personification of Jesus Christ. "The people of Sellers were sure that no one would come, no one would help and no one would care, but our United Methodist volunteers helped to prove that there are still good people in this world that will love and support those they don't even know."

For many homeowners, the Sellers blitz was the answer to fervent and desperate prayer. Most were forced to remain in their homes after the flood because they had nowhere else to go. Since October, many have had to cook on campsite burners and share toilets and showers.

Sellers Mayor Barbara Hopkins said the volunteers brought so much hope to her community.

"No one knew this town existed; it was forgotten," said Hopkins, whose own

Above, ERT member Russ Arant nails down a tarp. Below. Rev. Tim Rogers leads the group in prayer before work begins.

home burned down because the flood knocked over a power line. But thanks to the work of the UMC, she sees some very happy people in Sellers.

"This will make it a safe place to live, a haven for the families," Hopkins said. "The storm really took a toll on the whole town, but it made us get closer because we realized we need each other in Christ. It wasn't about you or me but about being about God."

—Jessica Brodie, editor
South Carolina United Methodist Advocate

Chapter 31

Spared the Wrath of Hurricane Irma
September 2017

South Carolina United Methodist Volunteers in Mission's Early Response Team started a response to Hurricane Irma on September 12, 2017, one day after the storm hit. By the grace of God, this state was spared a direct blow, and our teams responded to twelve damaged homes across our state instead of the thousands if we had received a direct hit.

ERT members started preparation for Hurricane Irma well in advance when it was a Category 5 in tandem with the South Carolina Conference of The United Methodist Church's Disaster Response Committee. Conference calls kept everyone abreast, and warnings along with vital information were sent out to all personnel.

After the storm, the committee immediately started assessing the situation, and ERTs went into action across the state. We have more than 300 ERT certified volunteers and seven disaster response trailers across our state.

By the grace of God, we were spared the kind of large-scale disaster we experienced the past two years, with many sites that our rebuild teams are still working on. ERT response was limited this time, as the number of damaged homes was much less than expected considering the strong tropical force winds and some flooding.

We received requests through various means, including county emergency managers, disaster response coordinators, local churches, and the state's 211 Information Line in conjunction with Crisis Clean Up, which is a system the South Carolina Emergency Management Division and South Carolina Volunteer Or-

ERT members work at a mobile home near Savannah that was damaged by Hurricane Irma.

ganizations Active in Disaster use.

We responded to various calls throughout the state, and several of our ERTs also responded to Florida and other states as needed.

One ERT response to Hurricane Irma found us at a destroyed mobile home in North, South Carolina, on September 14. The occupant of the home had thankfully sought shelter away from her home when a huge oak tree came crashing onto it and through the den, demolishing the home. Her access to the home and all her belongings was cut off by the debris and unsafe conditions, plus she was worried further storms would ruin everything she had left.

We cut egress routes out to the home, retrieved her belongings (including furniture and appliances), and relocated them to a warehouse in town for safekeeping. We also provided her with spiritual care including prayer.

The week of September 24 found us in the Savannah/Tybee Island, Georgia, areas performing chainsaw work and muck-out of six homes. Twelve volunteers worked two eleven-hour days and six volunteers worked an additional eight-hour day. On the first day we completed five chainsaw projects, three of which included heavy chainsaw work. At two of the locations, we performed roof work using tarps and tar.

On the second and third days, we mucked out a home on Tybee Island that had as much as twenty-six inches of salt water inside. The home, a duplex, had people living in both ends. We helped remove all their belongings and construct

At the man's request, Trudy Robinson reads scripture to a man staying in a flooded home on Tybee Island, Georgia.

a tent to temporarily store the good items while discarding most water-damaged appliances and furniture. We cleaned the homes by scrubbing and using a spray to stop mold.

We were able to pray with the survivors, as well as witness and share the gospel of Jesus Christ to them through our actions, through conversation, and through the reading of scripture to a few who asked us why we do what we do. We respond that it is a distinct honor and privilege to be used by God as his hands and feet, which gives us great fulfillment. Plus, you cannot out-give God. The more you give, the more you receive in true everlasting riches found only in Jesus Christ.

We stayed at the beautiful Wesley Gardens Retreat in Savannah where God's magnificent and splendid nature was ever-present. The South Georgia UMC Conference set us up nicely and, in a joint effort, we were able to provide much-needed aid using a database system called Crisis Clean-up in which all faith-based organizations, Red Cross, and state and federal agencies can input projects needing help. Also called the 211 information system, it is one of the main ways survivors can make their needs known by providing detailed information to 211, which then enters those needs into Crisis Clean-up. We are able to utilize the system before leaving on a mission or in the midst of a mission, as we did this time, calling back to our Assistant Coordinator Chuck Marshall and having him direct us to further needs and input the information on completed missions.

Our ERT volunteers came from all across the state and included myself and Rev. Fred Buchanan as team leaders, along with Trudy Robinson, Rev. Bob and Becky Allen, Hank Edens, Gary Smith, Bill Turner, Ray Mills, Steve Yano, and Felix and Misty Vazquez.

—*Billy Robinson*

Things Aren't Always What They Appear to Be

On September 27, 2017, on our response after Hurricane Irma to Tybee Island, we were staying at Wesley Gardens Retreat, a beautiful spot right on Shipyard Creek located near Tybee Island where Hurricane Irma had done a considerable amount of damage.

We were mucking out one man's house on an extremely hot and muggy day. On our second day there, I was going through some wet books, one of which was a Bible. The homeowner saw what I was doing and stopped me. Telling me he was dyslexic, he asked whether I would mind reading the Bible to him.

Eager to do so, I stopped working and started reading him the Bible, which was a very emotional and inspiring moment to me.

Little did I know that my husband, Billy Robinson, who was leading the response and was a good distance away, saw me just sitting there, doing nothing but reading. I found out later at an ERT training, when he laughed and told the story, that he thought I was just goofing off and could not understand why—until he discovered what and to whom I was reading.

We all have times when we look at people and situations and judge, but we still look back on this one and laugh.

Always, always give everyone the benefit of the doubt!

—*Trudy Robinson*

Chapter 32

Lessons from the Lord in Lithia
OCTOBER 8-12, 2017

October 8-12 was the last leg of our response to Hurricane Irma, which took us to Lithia, Florida, and areas south, where the eye of the hurricane came through.

Three South Carolina United Methodist Volunteers in Mission Early Response Teams with three ERT trailers and twenty-two wonderful, God-inspired volunteers responded. We stayed at Grace Community United Methodist Church in Lithia and were treated to a wide variety of meals, supplies, and hospitality by them and Hyde Park UMC in Tampa.

We had to do a lot of assessing in the various storm-affected areas ourselves along with good cooperation from Rev. Erik Ashley of Grace Community UMC and others, including Ward Smith of the South Carolina Conference, who was already in Florida helping train Floridians on setup methods for roofing projects.

We helped fifteen families by showing the love of Jesus to them through our actions, care, and concern. We worked on fifteen homes, providing everything from chainsaw work to tarps on storm-damaged roofs to mucking/cleaning out water-damaged homes. Several of the homes were in such dire need that it took an entire team two days to complete. We divided into three teams.

We know God placed the right people into each team as we heeded his direction and formation. It was obvious that this was the case, as two of the families we helped had close family or had previously lived in the same location of a team member from South Carolina working on their home.

There are always several touching stories with our missions that really tug at our heartstrings—people who are hurting with destroyed homes, lives, and

Crews cut away a tree that had fallen onto and into this Florida home.

dreams. People who need the love and hope that comes only through Jesus Christ. We have the honor and privilege to display that to them through our actions and prayers. Each time we become better people as God also works in our lives, teaching us his patience, faith, trust, and more.

Our ERTs worked extremely hard in extremely hot and even dangerous situations, bringing hope and joy to many people in need as we cut up massive trees that destroyed portions of homes and allowed rain, bugs, heat, mold, debris, etc. inside. Some still had no power after almost a month. At two homes, we cut out trees and removed debris so the power company would have access to reconnect

Volunteers tarp a storm-damaged roof in Lithia, Florida.

their electricity.

We were able to help make their homes safe, sanitary, and secure by cutting away the trees and limbs that were sometimes deep into their homes. We placed tarps on the severely damaged roofs and cleaned out flooded homes while providing mold remediation.

We also provided them with spiritual care including prayer.

South Carolina's ERT responders were Rev. Mike Evans, Heather Evans, Ed Weston, Bill and Elaine Turner, Dennis Beauford, Curtis Burnett, Chuck Marshall, Cherilynn Hewitt, Phil Griswold, Gus Meyers, Pat Coleman, Jill Evans, Rev. Jimmy Dillard, Jim Miller, Steven Bishop, Daniel "Danny" McKeown, Hugh Kight, Don and Kathy Beatty, Sue Miller, and me. As well, Ward Smith acted both as a recovery trainer and an ERT.

We were joined one day by Floridian Charlie Radigan, whom Rev. Mike Evans had trained on a mission to Tampa and West Palm Beach, Florida, the week prior. Evans trained more than one hundred Floridians on how to do muck out work.

—*Billy Robinson*

Chapter 33

Blessed and Grateful, not Lucky
October 24, 2017

Not long after many of South Carolina United Methodist Volunteers in Mission's Early Response Team members returned from helping hurricane-ravaged people in Florida, they were back at mission work again. This time they responded to Spartanburg on October 24, 2017, in the aftermath of a tornado that had devastated several neighborhoods the day prior. The tornado blocked access to homes with large debris and toppled trees onto and into several homes.

Massive numbers of downed trees and exposed roofs were the biggest problems after the tornado, leaving hundreds of homeowners desperate for help with cleanup.

Using three ERT trailers and a skid steer, more than twenty volunteers worked hard cutting out egress routes and removing fallen trees from five homes, including the home of Trey and Leslie Hendon, which had two big trees on their home and a huge pine tree blocking all access to the rear of the home. Their driveway was also blocked by a massive, twisted pile of downed trees. Leslie is the daughter of Rev. Paul Harmon, then-superintendent of the South Carolina United Methodist Conference's Spartanburg District. Both Paul and Leslie helped with the ERT response.

"I am so grateful," Trey Hendon said after ERTs cleared their homesite. "I could not have afforded or been able to do this on my own."

ERT personnel worked with passion and a strong Christian drive to complete the five homes before nightfall. Nathan Welch, the Upstate ERT coordinator, used his skid steer to move large volumes of debris, including helping push portions of one tree off a home.

Assistant Statewide ERT Coordinator and the Spartanburg District Disaster Response Coordinator Chuck Marshall coordinated the ERT response and also several additional responses to the damaged area over the next days. A total of

Above, volunteers clear a path to a house after the tornado in Spartanburg. Below, then-United Methodist Spartanburg District Superintendent Rev. Paul Harmon (left) helps an ERT member remove debris from a home and driveway.

twelve homes/families received aid and were helped to get their lives back to normal through the "Christian love in action" displayed by dozens of ERT volunteers from the Upstate and from the Orangeburg District.

One volunteer, Phil Griswold, said many people were surprised to find out he and some of the others had just returned from helping hurricane survivors in Florida, asking, "Why do you do it?"

Choking back tears, Griswold said, "It's just because we love them."

—*Billy Robinson*

Chapter 34

Long Distance Bright Rays of Hope
February 24-March 3, 2018

South Carolina United Methodist Volunteers in Mission Early Response Team sent a ten-person response to Puerto Rico from February 24 through March 3 to help the island after destruction from Hurricanes Irma and Maria. Seven ERT members from Mount Horeb United Methodist Church, Lexington, participated, including Nate Gibson as team leader, David Ivey, Jason Bost, Keith Fairchild, Nick Shelley, and Matt and Jessica Brodie. Other ERT members were Keith Rowland from Dorchester, Rev. Mike Evans from Abbeville, and me.

We were directed by the Methodist Church of Puerto Rico and the United Methodist Committee on Relief that our work would be all early response in nature, even though five months had gone by since the hurricanes had pounded the island.

Upon arrival, we found that most of the true ERT needs had been met in the area we were directed to, which was about one hour from San Juan in the areas of Arecibo and Hatillo. We were the first United Methodist mission team to help in the area after these hurricanes, and we stayed at a Methodist camp near Arecibo, which was nice but still had no electricity, and the roadway had been cut out just enough for our vehicles to access. The UMCOR coordinator for the area, Rubin, met us and stated it was his third week on the job.

Rubin said most of the true ERT work had been completed in the area except for some distant regions they were unsure about. We were directed to a home needing a tin roof, a muck out, some siding work, and painting. We were also sent to another needing some tear out and a tarp.

The island of Puerto Rico was hit by a double-whammy of storms that left much damage.

We completed those in two days and asked for more work. We put another tin roof on a home, plus exterior siding, and completed another tarp job on a second home.

The last day we made eight chest lockers for the Methodist camp for future teams to use.

It rained every day for a month until the day we started work, and then God directed all the rain around us. The last three days it did not rain at all. Temperatures were in the eighties for highs and upper sixties for lows. The mosquitoes were not as bad as we were told they were going to be, but we did use mosquito netting.

The UMCOR leader for the state/territory met with us one afternoon and was impressed at all we had accomplished and took a lot of photos of our work to try to get future teams. Spanish is the main language, and we had an interpreter with us. A transit van was all we had to transport us and the materials from job sites, though they did deliver the bulk of our supplies to two of our sites. A Home Depot store was within fifteen minutes of us, and we shopped there on several occasions. We had hoped there would be a warehouse filled with work tools and various supplies at all three of the Methodist camps, but there were very little supplies. If the majority of the team members had not brought construction tools and battery-powered tools, we would have only gotten half of our work completed. We did leave a good portion of our tools there.

They did not have a construction coordinator to stay at a location but only to

Nate Gibson nails down roofing material on a house in Hatillo, Puerto Rico.

direct us where to go. Two Honda generators donated by Samaritan's Purse were there for us to use.

Our team did have a good experience and was filled with energetic people with good construction and ERT skills plus wonderful personalities. We even had the opportunity to help a man on the street one day as we were driving back to the camp from our worksite. We saw a man nearly collapsed on the street corner, and all of us jumped out of the van to see if he needed help. We checked his blood pressure and glucose levels. While some of us were working on him, the rest of the team was praying. His friend came by, and even though we didn't speak the language, we were able to convince him to take the man to the hospital. Every experience we go on, an awesome thing like that happens that just stands out.

The team shined forth with Jesus's love into the darkness of a major disaster and left bright rays of hope and love for all to see and feel.

It was our distinct honor and privilege to represent the hands and feet of Jesus and our state of South Carolina to hurting people, and we all came back as richer and more fulfilled Christians.

I believe it is a good thing that we from South Carolina sent a team to help from such a long distance, and the people were very grateful. There is a lot of need there.

—Billy Robinson

An Opportunity to Witness

Sometimes, we find ourselves going on a mission trip without really understanding why. That's what happened with Rev. Mike Evans, who was on the Puerto Rico trip yet found himself with misgivings, wondering why the team was going so far away to help people in need when there were so many in need in our home state.

Evans got his answer right at the start of the trip, on the flight to Puerto Rico.

As he settled into his aisle seat, he noticed what he called a "scary looking" man sitting near him by the window. The man looked unapproachable, with his window shade pulled down and his hat pulled low, and Evans wondered whether the man was dangerous.

But the man turned to Nate Gibson, Evans' fellow ERT member, and asked him why so many people were wearing green shirts. The team was all wearing their green ERT T-shirts displaying the logo and motto, "Christian love in action."

"He looked at Nate and said, 'What's with all these green shirts you got going on here?' and Nate said, 'We're going to Puerto Rico to help out with storm relief, this is the ERT, and we feel like God is calling us to do this. We prayed about it.' And the man says, 'Well, tell me about your God.' And that's when Nate punched me and said, 'Preacher, it's your turn.'"

Right there on that airplane, after telling the man about Jesus, Evans said he got on his knees in between Nate and the man—who then accepted Jesus Christ as his savior.

They got the man's phone number and found out he was about to have gallbladder surgery. So a few days later, on the morning of his surgery, Evans got up early, called the man, and prayed with him before his surgery.

"And I knew for a fact why God had called us on that mission trip," Evans said.

Chapter 35

United Methodists Help Puerto Rico Rise
February 24-March 3, 2018

Driving through San Juan and into the mountains of northern Puerto Rico, it's hard to tell what is hurricane damage versus storm-exposed poverty.

Two-story concrete houses and mural-painted businesses stand strong alongside half-tattered rubble and buildings with blue-tarp roofs. Still others are just a crumpled shell of iron bars and decay. Litter-strewn patches of grass share space with grazing cows, horses, and goats. A giant crushed-metal structure fills the next field over.

And everywhere, amid the wreckage and the rebuild, Puerto Rican flags wave proudly.

Almost six months after the island was hit by a double-whammy of storms—Hurricane Irma September 6-7, then Hurricane Maria September 20—the flags represent a symbol of strength, like a Phoenix rising from the ashes. Even as many are still without electricity. Even as stores stay shuttered and jobs remain scarce.

"*Puerto Rico Se Levanta*," the bumper stickers read—Puerto Rico Rises Up.

Ten South Carolina United Methodist Volunteers in Mission Early Response Team members, including myself, spent one week recently as a rebuild and construction team in Puerto Rico, helping with materials purchased by the Methodist Church of Puerto Rico with the support of the United Methodist Committee on Relief from The Home Depot. The team spent time in Arecibo and Hatillo doing construction on four houses and a Methodist camp February 24 to March 3.

Three of the four houses became livable again because of our efforts.

"This team represented the best of the South Carolina Annual Conference, not in terms of who we were, but in terms of how we worked and how we loved," said team leader Nate Gibson. "More than any roof we installed or house we painted, we represented hope and a reminder that God and his people are the foundation upon which Puerto Rico will rise again."

Theodore Warnock, UMCOR's missionary of special projects, said he helped unload a truck of materials on Saturday and, by Monday, the South Carolina team was using them to put a roof on a house.

"There was no delay in making a home habitable for living," he said. "It warms your heart knowing what you're doing is being able to move a family back in. Just—wow."

Ruben Velez, director of logistics for the Methodist Church of Puerto Rico, said the island is finally transitioning from response to recovery and rebuild. The South Carolina team was one of the sixty volunteer work teams in the queue that Velez and his team are working to match with home sites.

"We don't see ourselves as people that know everything. We need everything, and we welcome everything," Velez said, from materials to volunteers to money.

Velez said as Maria came in from the southeast, it touched near a Methodist camp in Patillas, cut diagonally through the island near another Methodist camp, and exited in the northwest, near the Methodist camp in Arecibo. A strong Methodist presence runs throughout the path of the storm, something Velez hopes will guide their recovery.

The Methodist Church of Puerto Rico's recovery strategy follows much the same path, using local churches to help recognize the damage with case managers spiraling out from there, going house by house, place by place. They are starting near the two coastal camps and hope to head into the center of the island in a few weeks.

"I am privileged to be here," Velez said, hugging one homeowner, then turning to talk shop with a construction team, switching from English to Spanish and back again. "You see that lady's face? You see the neighbor's smile? We don't see this kind of support and love. This is God's love making itself flesh and blood again. This is Emmanuel—God with us."

Rev. Sergio Valentin, pastor of Iglesia Metodista El Calvario, the South Carolina team's host church, has worked tirelessly to helped identify home sites. The congregation is focusing on helping the unchurched community first, putting church and congregation needs last. And as they and so many others have stepped up to help, Valentin says he's seen God's hands with Puerto Rico.

"The experience has been an inspiration. Even people who don't know us have come here to help us, all part of God's hands to help here on earth," Valentin said, raising his eyes to the steeple high above his circa-1903 church. "Dios bendiga

Keith Rowland and Jessica Brodie measure a cut at a house in Puerto Rico.

(God's blessing)."

For the homeowners, the blessing—and the rising up—cannot happen soon enough.

One mother of two, Yenitza, lost everything she owned between Irma and Maria. Her Hatillo house was the first place the South Carolina team worked when they arrived.

"Destroida," she said, gesturing to the roofless second story above her head—destroyed. Only the bathroom and part of one wall are still standing, the rest of her belongings piled in a heap by the roadside. One of her daughter's shoes pokes out beneath a rusted sheet of metal roofing and a rotted, waterlogged length of plywood. She's getting government funds to rebuild her house once it's cleared out; the South Carolina team gutted the structure in preparation.

Another Hatillo homeowner, Ada Villanueva Cadelaria, brought her two children to live next door with her mother after Maria hit. Thanks to the South Carolina team's efforts, she not only has a new metal roof over her small house but also fresh paint and wood trim, and by the time they left was gathering furniture to move back home.

She can barely express how she feels about the assistance she received. "Es genial," she says simply, staring at the brightly painted one-story structure, chickens and their chicks darting across the path at her feet as she gropes for the words—it feels great.

Gibson said he and his team were honored to play a role in helping the island rebuild—and to help Puerto Rico *se levanta*.

"It was humbling to be so early into the rebuilding effort and see genuine hope from everybody—those receiving our assistance and those who just saw us there—because it gave flesh to the se levanta slogan they have adopted, and you could tell it gave them hope that they weren't going to have to rise again by themselves."

Angel de Jesus, twenty-eight, said between the shortage of food, water, gasoline, electricity and basic communication, everyone on the island suffered, even those lucky enough not to experience damage at their own home. But he said the beautiful part has been watching how the people came together to help each other—and now getting the chance to see people come from far away to help, too.

"It's going to be a long, long time to rebuild—block by block, step by step, maybe many years, but the help is welcome," de Jesus said. "We feel relieved you are here. God brings the help."

Nicole Mendéz, eighteen, also said she is grateful for the teams beginning to travel to Puerto Rico to assist in the rebuild and recovery effort. Her family had some scary times throughout the past few months, particularly right after the storm; her twenty-two-year-old sister is diabetic, and without power, they had to rely on a generator to refrigerate her insulin — difficult given the scarcity of gasoline.

But Mendéz said she felt God's presence throughout, and she still feels it now, watching and helping as others join in to help Puerto Rico rise again.

"People were desperate, you couldn't find things you needed, my mom would just wake up and listen to the radio and cry, but I felt very calm. Then and now, I felt reassured by God. We are going to survive somehow. Somehow, there is life; there is hope."

Like the Phoenix rising from the ashes, Mendéz said, "We will move forward."

Billy Robinson, South Carolina's ERT coordinator, said he'd thought the trip would involve mainly early response work, such as tarping and muck-out. It turned out to be more rebuild work with a little ERT work mixed in, but they still had a wonderful experience.

"The team shined forth with Jesus's love into the darkness of a major disaster and left bright rays of hope and love for all to see and feel," he said. "It was our distinct honor and privilege to represent the hands and feet of Jesus and South Carolina to hurting people."

— *Jessica Brodie, editor*
South Carolina United Methodist Advocate

Chapter 36

Thank God for Volunteers
September-November 2018

South Carolina United Methodist Volunteers in Mission's Early Response Team started preparation for hurricanes Florence and Michael well in advance, along with all of South Carolina's United Methodist Disaster Response Committee.

After the storms, ERTs deployed across the state. By now, we have more than 400 ERT-certified volunteers and seven disaster response trailers across our state. We were spared a big-scale disaster across most of the state but did have wind damage in several counties. Then came massive flooding in both North and South Carolina, prompting major ERT responses in Cheraw, Bennettsville, McColl, Dillon, Marion, Conway, Myrtle Beach, and many points in-between.

As soon as the storms blew through, we started responses to wind damage in Orangeburg County on September 17, the day after Hurricane Florence came ashore in North Carolina. Over the next weeks, we responded to several other areas of our state after wind damage from Florence and Michael. We had to wait until the rivers crested and floodwaters receded before we could safely respond.

We first responded in the Marion area with twenty-six ERT volunteers and three ERT trailers on September 23. Marion United Methodist Church hosted our teams in a home on their property that had been abandoned for eight years. They quickly got utilities, heating and air, appliances, supplies, and the house overall in good shape to house our teams over the next months. They, along with several other churches, also fed our teams and made us feel extremely welcome and right at home. Heading up the hospitality and helping coordinate our response was then-Marion District Superintendent Rev. Tim Rogers and Marion District Disaster Coordinators Rev. Randy Bowers and Brian Nolan. Churches also housed our teams out of Cheraw, McColl, and Conway and were vital to our responses.

Our ERT core group of volunteer leaders led the way. Through their many hours of intense struggles, frustration, planning, personal emergencies, coordination, fi-

Felix Vazquez uses a chainsaw to clear debris.

nances, love, care, and concern, many volunteers, teams, and equipment were put into action, and we had a well-coordinated disaster response amid much chaos. Leaders included Chuck Marshall, Rev. Mike Evans, Matt Brodie, Terry Rawls, Brian Nolan, Marion District Superintendent Tim Rogers, Rev. Ken Phelps, Don Beatty, Rev. Fred Buchanan, Rev. Frank Copeland and Mayo Collier. Then came all the wonderful and extremely faithful volunteers and team leaders.

We had six major responses that consisted of multiple teams each time and many other single team responses to various disaster sites. Most of the response was to flooded homes and structures needing roof work, such as tarps, including several churches.

Aaron Meadows of the Charleston Wesley Foundation and Phelps, the Pee Dee ERT coordinator, led one major response. They led fifty college students to a one-day blitz in Horry County. The majority of the students were from The Citadel and had taken the ERT training in Charleston on September 22 taught by Buchanan and myself. They were provided free stay at a resort in Myrtle Beach owned by ERT Assistant Pee Dee Coordinator Gary Smith. The group mucked out five homes and did various types of ERT work and repairs on two additional homes.

Bragg Williams nails down a tarp on a severely damaged home near Norway, South Carolina.

In all, more than 160 volunteers worked approximately 3,800 hours providing Christian love in action to survivors in dire need of help.

Each volunteer went home a better and richer person having grown in their faith and appreciation of God's grace, mercy, and love for all.

—Billy Robinson

Chapter 37

God's Teams Move Mountains
March 4-6, 2019

On Monday, March 4, 2019, a South Carolina United Methodist Volunteers in Mission Early Response Team responded to Columbia, South Carolina, in the aftermath of an EF1 tornado that hit a neighborhood on Saluda River Road the Sunday afternoon before.

That Sunday evening, March 3, an entire neighborhood saw just how forceful and damaging a tornado could be as it toppled many trees, some of which were huge and several of those onto homes. On Saluda River Road, a huge pine tree not only hit a home but split it as it violently crashed through. A man's life was spared by inches as the massive tree landed on a couch, trapping him inside until a neighbor could clear enough debris for him to get out.

Monday found him with some family members plus the owner fervently trying to clear away the massive debris out of his home so he could retrieve and salvage his belongings. Debris also had to be moved off three vehicles that were severely damaged.

We joined them and formed a powerful team through which God moved a mountain of debris and restored hope and warm love to the residents and homeowners. The overall team flowed well together, starting with debris removal off the vehicles, then to access into the home, where all valuables and belongings were removed and safely stored.

It was a beautiful sight to see such a caring and loving gathering of volunteer strangers uniting as one to help people in need.

Rewards for helping others as God calls us to do are something you cannot put a price tag on. They are priceless and give fulfillment as nothing else does.

ERT volunteers included Don and Kathy Beatty, Felix and Misty Vazquez, Trudy Robinson, Rev. Mike Evans, Dan Dowbridge, Rev. Monica Tilley, Bill and Elaine Turner, and myself as team leader.

—Billy Robinson

Billy Robinson hauls off tree limbs, above. Below, Kathy Beatty removes debris as Robinson and Don Beatty hook the trunk of a tree to a tractor run by the homeowner.

Chapter 38

The Church Being the Church It Is Called to Be
July 5, 2019

On Thursday afternoon, July 4, 2019, straight-line winds blew through Greenwood, knocking trees onto homes and driveways across the community.

A South Carolina United Methodist Volunteers in Mission Early Response Team stepped up to help in the aftermath, sending volunteers to help neighbors in need.

One of the homes belonged to a man with physical disabilities who had downed trees, including one dangerously close to his house.

The team gathers with the massive tree they removed from a homeowner's yard.

The driveway was completely impassable when ERT volunteers arrived.

"This handicapped gentlemen needed some help, and he reached out to the county and the county to us, and with us trying to be Christlike, here we are," said Rev. Mike Evans.

The driveway was completely impassable when ERT volunteers arrived, and they got the driveway cleared and the trees removed.

Evans said helping people through ERT work is a blessing, both for those they serve and for the volunteers themselves.

"We always think of the church as inside four walls but this is bringing the church to the people," Evans said.

Kathy Beatty added, "It's a blessing to be able to help people. You don't have to have special skills, just the ability and willingness to help your neighbor."

This is the church in action while being the church God calls it to be. The rewards for following Jesus's commands to help people in need are priceless. We are being God's hands and feet to others during their times of need.

—*Billy Robinson*

Chapter 39

Cold and Snowy Weather, Warm and Loving Hearts
February 8, 2020

On the morning of February 6, 2020, an EF1 tornado hit Spartanburg, South Carolina, near the West Gate Mall, damaging homes, destroying trees and neighborhoods, and causing power outages and much chaos.

South Carolina United Methodist Volunteers in Mission Early Response Team members were allowed into the danger zones Saturday morning, February 8. After an informative meeting with Spartanburg Emergency Management, nineteen ERT volunteers and three ERT trailers were deployed to Zones 1 and 2 of the tornado's path as determined by management.

As with most tornadoes, some homes had a lot of tree and roof damage, while others only yards away had very little or none. The temperature was in the thirties, so many people had left their homes overnight because they had no power or heat and returned in the morning to start clean-up and check on neighbors. Several were returning to check on their pets.

We focused on clearing debris out of driveways, making access routes into people's homes, and placing tarps on damaged roofs.

We cleared debris and trees off two driveways of single mothers, who had no means of acquiring or paying for help. Help was available if you had a lot of money, stated several people who had companies coming by offering to clear their drives and get trees off their homes for large sums of money, which most could not afford.

One man who came back to his home to feed his pets told us about a company wanting $6,000 to cut and clear several medium-sized trees off his driveway and several leaning toward his home. We completed the job for him for free with one six-person team in two hours.

Rev. John Elmore nails down a tarp in the snow on a tornado-damaged roof in Spartanburg while team members on the ground cut trees.

One lady teared up when we showed up to help take two big trees off her home and tarp her damaged roof. Her home had been broken into and ransacked several days prior. Some companies had offered to help remove the tree and tarp her roof for large sums of money, which she did not have—especially after being robbed. She said she and her grandmother had prayed tearful and emotional prayers for help the night before. Then God sent us in his mighty grace and mercy. Wow—how wonderful and awesome it is to be used by God. It brings a fulfillment, purpose, and meaning to life that nothing else can come close to.

We were requested to eat lunch at a Red Cross shelter, where they had graciously prepared a hot meal for us and made us feel right at home. The cold day got a lot colder as snow began to fall, which made disaster scenes appear beautiful amid the splendor of God's beauty.

We bundled up and went back to work in the snow, which accumulated around an inch, making conditions a bit more hazardous and miserable, especially while placing tarps on roofs. But at the end of the day, with our hands and feet freezing, we had completed work on six homes while completing our assigned zones.

One team, led by our District Disaster Coordinator Chuck Marshall, went back out on Friday, February 14. They cut up and cleared downed trees in the yard of the parsonage for St. James United Methodist Church on Arrowhead Circle, plus two other homes, one of which had a giant white oak to clear.

Once again, we are so thankful and grateful to God for allowing us to be used in his service in such life-changing ways. Glory to God in the highest.

—*Billy Robinson*

Chapter 40

A Disaster Within a Disaster
April 13, 2020

Less than a month after the COVID-19 pandemic shuttered schools, churches, and businesses, causing a global health crisis, South Carolina United Methodist Volunteers in Mission Early Response Teams were called upon to help in Christian love in yet another disaster to strike this state.

In the early morning of April 13, tornadoes swept across South Carolina, leveling homes, claiming lives, yet providing an opportunity for people of faith to step up as God's hands and feet.

The National Weather Service confirmed at least twenty tornadoes touched down in South Carolina in the wee hours after Easter Sunday. It was the biggest tornado outbreak in the state since 1984. Nine people were killed, 150 homes destroyed, nearly 1,500 homes damaged, and almost 300,000 homes lost power. Several of the tornadoes were classified as EF3 twisters, meaning their winds were as high as 165 miles per hour.

That afternoon, ERTs sprang into action, with major aid rendered in the three hardest-hit pockets of the state: Orangeburg County, Seneca and Clemson, and the Walterboro/Estill/Hampton community.

"At 6:04 a.m., I received a tornado warning call over my North Volunteer Fire/Rescue radio," said Billy Robinson, South Carolina's ERT coordinator and assistant chief of North Volunteer Fire Department. "At 6:19 a.m. we were called out to our first entrapment call to 449 Sharpe Road out of North for two people trapped inside an overturned mobile home by an EF3 tornado. We—including Rev. Richard Toy of North UMC, who is also a volunteer firefighter and chaplain—responded immediately in pouring rain and hazardous conditions toward

ERT members rescued two severely injured tornado survivors from this destroyed mobile home in North.

the trapped couple, but massive debris piles of large trees entwined in downed power lines and poles had to be cut out and pathways cleared before we could reach them."

Ambulances could not make it through because of low-hanging power lines and trees, so crews had to make their own access in their personal trucks. Two severely injured survivors, Devin and Amanda Thompson, were freed from their demolished mobile home, placed on spine boards, then put into the back of Robinson's personal truck and rushed to a waiting ambulance. Devin said he saw the tornado coming and hollered for everyone to get into a bathtub, which they did, and he laid on top of them. The tornado flipped the mobile home at least three times, injuring Devin and Amanda, but their two children walked away in good shape.

"We were then off to another location where three survivors were freed from another destroyed home, and we made access to other injured survivors. Unfortunately, one married couple died in the area we were working," Robinson added. "It was like we were living out a chaotic, scary, unrealistic dream. It was hard for our minds to comprehend what we were seeing and experiencing. We were literally living a real nightmare."

In Seneca, tornadoes started just after 4 a.m., and within the first hour, local agencies were responding to address emergencies within a defined grid established by an up and functioning command post, reported Jill Evans.

"The word 'overwhelmed' doesn't describe the magnitude of the debris field of power poles, power lines, trees and parts of buildings making navigation within

Teams worked to clear debris, cut trees off homes, and tarp damaged roofs after the storm.

the zone difficult," Evans said.

Matt Brodie, then-disaster response coordinator for the South Carolina Conference of The United Methodist Church, said the church has truly stepped up to help.

"Areas around our state have been devastated by tornadoes and strong storms. Families around the state have lost homes, jobs, and even loved ones," Brodie said. "But the people of The United Methodist Church continue to bring hope in the form of volunteers willing to help. Our early response teams have been working to clear debris, cut trees off homes, and tarp damaged roofs."

Robinson called the outpouring of help "a wonderful, loving and caring response to the deadly and very devastating" disaster.

"Many very challenging and difficult situations were faced and overcome with God's power, strength, resources and insight," Robinson said.

While COVID-19 was a real threat that kept some responders away because of health concerns and fears, those who did respond took special precautions and made huge progress, he said.

"COVID-19 was a new fear among us with a lot of unknown consequences," Robinson said. "It added a scary factor to our responses, though we did not allow it to stop us or slow us down much. We used safety precautions and continued as we knew Jesus would have us to do and rested our fears and hopes in Jesus alone."

Orangeburg County response

ERT teams went immediately into action in Orangeburg County April 13, the morning of the storm, alongside fire, rescue, emergency management ser-

An ERT member cuts away a downed tree.

vices, law enforcement and others.

On Preserver Road, Robinson said, they were able to rescue five people, taking more than an hour to cut through the debris.

A command post was set up at the Piggly Wiggly in Neeses. Emergency and fire services continued with a coordinated search and damage assessment throughout the morning into early afternoon. There, the F3 tornado was 700 yards wide and cut a path thirty miles long, Robinson said, with fourteen homes destroyed and seventeen with major damage. Many other homes had moderate to slight damage.

ERT members came to help right away from Greenwood, Summerville, and North. They started by cutting out access to a man on oxygen with various other health issues and no power. Fire personnel and law enforcement worked side by side with ERT members and had him freed, with a generator on the way, within forty-five minutes.

"We then moved onto cutting trees off of homes and placing tarps on damaged roofs," Robinson said. "Each family had exceptional stories of storm survival, including the first people rescued in the early morning, as we tarped a shed and helped move debris for them with family members as the parents were still in the hospital."

The family had heard the tornado warning, he said, and placed a mattress over the teenagers. Just as the parents got a mattress on top of them, they and the mattress were lifted into the air. The mobile home rolled several times. The teenagers were unhurt, but the parents both had serious injuries.

The following day, ERT members helped cut a tree off an RV for the family; it was pulled into the newly cleared position of their old home. Community and family volunteers poured into the devastated site and retrieved many valuables for the devastated family, including three vehicles from under the trailer's remains. Bonnie Robinson and Michael Hughes from North UMC came with sandwiches and fixings for lunch, which they continued to do for several days. They were followed by others bringing food to various sites where volunteers had gathered to follow the golden rule and truly "love their neighbors as themselves" despite the coronavirus.

"One minister and his family barely escaped death as four family members hunkered down in their bathroom and constantly prayed to God for the winds and damage to go away and leave them unhurt," Robinson said. "A massive tree literally split their home in two and missed crashing through the bathroom by inches. No one was injured and all were very thankful to be alive."

More ERT began to respond across the state the next day, April 14, in North—cutting out egress routes to homes, removing trees off of homes and placing tarps on damaged roofs—as well as in the Seneca-Clemson area and the Lowcountry.

Nearby United Methodist and other churches and individuals offered housing and meals.

"It was like we were living out a chaotic, scary, unrealistic dream. It was hard for our minds to comprehend what we were seeing and experiencing," Robinson said. "We were literally living a real nightmare."

Seneca-Clemson response

More than 400 UMVIM and ERT volunteers responded after tornadoes swept through the Upstate.

An EF3 tornado touched down on the west side of Seneca and cut a half-mile-wide by sixteen-mile-long path of unimaginable destruction across the city of Seneca and the eastern part of Oconee County, Evans reported.

"By evening civic organizations, local churches, construction crews and arborists had flooded the area providing food and clothing and starting the cleanup," Evans said.

In the midst of the pandemic, relief volunteers found themselves called to serve others in Seneca. ERTs mobilized Monday and arrived Tuesday from Spartanburg, Greenwood, Anderson, and Columbia districts, working hand-in-hand with the Caney Fork River District ERTs, who arrived from the Tennessee Conference with trucks, volunteers, and heavy equipment in tow. Community volunteers also lined up to help.

Ann Hope and St. Mark UMCs were in the center of the disaster zone, Evans said, and their parking lots were used to feed people and provide bathrooms all while having no power to the buildings.

"Our purpose is to love one another and although the destruction and the personal losses are heartbreaking, the outpouring of help and support from the community has been incredible," Evans said. "By the end of the week, we became family after spending 24/7 living, working, and crying together. The Christian Life Center was the refuge where out-of-town volunteers bunked for the week. A volunteer commented after working the zone, 'This has been the best and hardest week of my life.'"

Evans said while the landscape of the area will be forever changed, so will the hearts of the people.

"This storm should provide a great reminder that you must be prepared and have a plan in place before the weather alert sounds. In fact, because this tornado was moving at sixty miles per hour across the ground, with sustained winds of 165 miles per hour, many didn't have time to make it into their shelter area from the time their phone warning system sounded," she said.

Stephen Turner was the Seneca Disaster lead; Chuck Marshall led a team from the Spartanburg District; Phil Griswold led a five-person team from New Beginnings UMC in Boiling Springs; Rev. John Elmore Jr. led a team from the Greenwood District; and Nick Shelly led a seven-person team from the Columbia District Lexington ERT Team. An eight-person team also came from the Tennessee Conference.

Walterboro/Estill/Hampton response

Rev. Fred Buchanan headed up the response in the Lowcountry and handled a big chainsaw and tarp disaster response in Varnville that took several days.

Buchanan's team was not able to get into the worst-hit areas until Tuesday after the storm and started work on Wednesday doing mainly chainsaw work clearing driveways and access to homes.

—*By Jessica Brodie, Jill Evans, and Billy Robinson*

Chapter 41

God's Guiding Hand of Safety
September and October 2020

South Carolina United Methodist Volunteers in Mission Early Response Teams responded to a continuous, desperate request for help along much of the Gulf Coast after Hurricanes Laura, Sally, and Delta.

Our first response was through a five-person team to Mobile and Dauphin Island, Alabama, in the week following Hurricane Sally. The next week, two additional South Carolina ERT teams— consisting of thirteen volunteers and two disaster response trailers—headed to the same region. Teams were led by Rev. Fred Buchanan of St. Paul's United Methodist Church in Orangeburg, Billy Robinson of North UMC in North, and Rev. Mike Evans of Edgefield UMC in Edgefield.

The response included a lot of dangerous storm-damaged trees that needed to be removed from structures and yards as they posed serious hazards to the homes and property owners. God's vision and powerful hand guided and kept all of us safe, giving us the proper equipment and knowledge to safely handle all the challenging disaster responses.

We placed tarps on three homes and one shed; shingled a portion of one church roof and two separate church sheds, repaired one tin roof, placed tar and caulk on one mobile home, and completed ten big chainsaw jobs.

There were sad stories and dire cries for help as many people did not have the funds or means to remove the big fallen trees or patch their leaking roofs. One man had suffered a stroke and was desperately trying to cut away portions of a huge tree with a small saw to make access to his shed and property. Another lady, who is a member of a local UMC, sustained major damage to her property from

David Bryant, left, moves debris to the roadside as Steve Bishop and Rev. Mike Evans use chainsaws to cut up a big tree that Hurricane Sally blew down.

fallen trees, including big limbs on and over her home and a big tree dangerously positioned over an out building, blocking access to her yard. In the immediate aftermath of Hurricane Sally's devastation, her son was killed in a wreck near Myrtle Beach, and she went to help coordinate and attend his funeral. When she returned home on our last day there, she found someone had looted much of her belongings. We were able to help her on the evening of our last day and were joined by several of her church members and the pastor.

All glory goes to God, as we were able to be used by him to accomplish these tasks and most importantly show the love and care of Jesus to all hurting, hopeless, and stressed out people we came into contact with.

The bishop, district superintendent, and other church leaders from the Alabama-West Florida Conference of the UMC asked us to teach chainsaw safety classes to them and also provide them with information so they can establish ERT teams in their conference. Several of us taught two classes in the late afternoons after two work days in the Mobile, Alabama, and Pensacola, Florida, areas.

Rebuild continued all along the Gulf Coast and inland for years to come.

—*Billy Robinson*

Chapter 42

The Joy of the Lord Jesus is My Strength
April 5-8, 2021

Our South Carolina United Methodist Volunteers in Mission Early Response Team responded to a dire call for help in Alabama after several deadly tornadoes ravaged their state, killing five people, injuring many, plus wreaking havoc on homes, farms, and businesses.

A fifteen-member South Carolina ERT team along with two disaster response trailers responded to Bibb County below Birmingham, working out of Brent United Methodist Church in Brent, Alabama, April 5-8, 2021.

In the wake of a huge EF3 tornado, the disaster area was more than a mile and a quarter wide in spots. It spanned four counties and caused massive devastation all along its hundred-mile path through mainly rural countryside.

Brent UMC showed us Christian hospitality, providing us with housing in their church building and three great meals a day. Chris Ackerman is the Alabama-West Florida Conference disaster response coordinator whom we met in November 2020 when we responded to the Mobile area after several hurricanes, including Hurricane Sally. Ackerman and two South Carolina ERT members scouted and assessed the disaster areas early April 5. Then we were off and running as God's hands and feet to hurting and emotionally distraught people.

We split into two teams and over the next several days provided emotional, spiritual, and physical aid to many survivors. A couple of Alabama ERT members also joined us, using their tractors and chainsaws to help, including Rev. Thomas Leggett of Brent UMC who only a month prior had a tornado destroy his homestead.

Many people had miraculous stories of how they escaped death by getting to the centermost portions of their homes, leaving their mobile homes and seeking more substantial structures, or simply being away from their homes when the horrific tornadoes hit. One man told about how he laid across his children as a tornado tore off portions of his roof, which we tarped to prevent rain from destroying the inside. Another man almost unbelievably rode out a direct hit of the EF3 tornado that obliterated his home around him, leaving him basically unhurt on his couch in the middle of a pile of rubble that used to be his home.

A family came up to us thanking us for coming so far to help, though we were unable to help them as their home was crushed by several huge trees. Graciously, they escaped harm. A woman who was physically and mentally stressed by the disaster ministered as much to us as we did to her while helping her cope with the

Above, Dan Dowbridge runs a chainsaw cutting storm debris out of a roadway to a home. Below, the team was able to cut access to two pigs trapped and in dire need of water and food.

aftermath that left six trees through her home. God's joy was ever present in and through her. She was unwilling to leave her devastated home yet, so we tarped the portion she was living in and made it inhabitable for now.

We cut out downed trees and removed debris to help families salvage their family goods, which in most cases were strewn over several hundred yards and intertwined among a wide variety of storm debris. In one rather unusual case, we were able to cut out egress to two pigs trapped under debris and in dire need of water and food.

We prayed with many survivors and left scripture care items with them. We also provided major chainsaw work to six homes, including cutting out access to pump houses, egress routes and roads, and trees off homes. We tarped five homes and helped survivors start pick up the pieces of their household goods, and more

Above, the team gathers for a smile. Below, the disaster area was more than a mile and a quarter wide in spots.

importantly, their lives.

We have responded to these types of disasters multiple times a year throughout our seventeen years of ERT responses throughout the Southeast. Every time it is so encouraging to see the best come out in people as neighbors come together to help each other and Christian churches spring into action and become "the church" Jesus calls us to be. It's not a church of brick and mortar but blood, sweat, tears, and love.

South Carolina ERT responders included myself along with Rev. Fred Buchanan, Darrel Briggs, Chuck Marshall, Rev. John Elmore, Jim Smith, Curtis Burnett, Rev. Jimmy Dillard, Worth Adams, Wade Dickens, Dan Dowbridge, Frank Grambling, Phil Griswold, Jerry Pullen, and Michael Hughes. Just as important were all the people praying for us and financially supporting our missions, plus people like Rev. Mike Evans. Evans helped coordinate the mission, then had his gallbladder taken out two days prior causing him and his daughter Ashley to miss the trip, although they were present in spirit and prayer.

To God be all glory, honor, and praise.

—Billy Robinson

Chapter 43

The Love and Presence of Jesus in Vance
July 16, 2021

On July 16, 2021, an eleven-person South Carolina United Methodist Volunteers in Mission Early Response Team responded to a desperate cry for help after a big hackberry tree had crashed into the end of a mobile home during a storm July 13.

The tree penetrated four feet into the home with its huge limbs perched dangerously over the rest of the home.

Orangeburg County Emergency Services Director Billy Staley contacted me for help, and a team was formed of ERT members from across the state. ERT Team Leader Rev. John Elmore had just moved into the parsonage of Holly Hill United Methodist Church when the storm hit. He did an assessment of the damaged home on July 14 and coordinated with homeowner Lashanda White to get her the help she and her family needed. Power was shut off to the home until the tree could be removed and the home could be deemed safe.

Elmore reached out to his church congregation to provide aid to the family, as well. Church member Michael Dennis brought a dump truck and hauled off several loads of debris. Other members brought drinks and rehabilitation supplies that helped us through the demanding and dangerous work on a hot and muggy day.

ERT members divided into three crews including roofing, ground, and debris removal. The roofing crew methodically cut the dangerous limbs hanging over the home using a pole saw with precise coordination from the ground crew, who had a rope attached to the limbs being cut. In perfect precision, they would pull it away from the home as it was cut into. The debris was loaded onto the dump

Jim Miller cuts a tree trunk out of a home as Felix Vazquez hammers in a wedge.

truck and hauled off. The roof crew faced some challenging obstacles when it got down to cutting the tree trunk from inside the home without causing further damage. A Fred Device was used to help keep tension off of the tree trunk.

After all of the tree was removed, the roof was tarped to encompass the damaged end of the home.

We prayed before and after with the family and left them with cross pendants and scripture including John 3:16. They asked for extras for other relatives and friends. One family member plans to attend our next ERT class. He stated, "I want to help others in need just as y'all have helped our family. Today, we have felt the love and presence of Jesus!"

—*Billy Robinson*

Chapter 44

Lifting Praises to Jesus After Hurricane Ida
September 2021

The South Carolina United Methodist Volunteers in Mission Early Response Team had a productive disaster response mission in and around the Ponchatoula, Louisiana, area and one in Pass Christian, Mississippi, after the devastating effects of Hurricane Ida.

A Category 4 storm, Hurricane Ida struck August 29, 2021. It was the second most damaging and intense hurricane in Louisiana history behind Hurricane Katrina. Wind speeds of 147 miles per hour shredded trees and homes in the Ponchatoula area, leaving chaos behind.

Our thirteen-person ERT team had boots on the ground hard at work three days after receiving the call for help. We responded from September 6-11 with many chainsaws and supplies, including a fully equipped disaster response trailer, skid steer, and mini excavator. We touched many lives, while our lives were also touched by tears of joy and high, loving emotions.

Survivors were devastated physically, mentally, and financially. Many lost everything they owned. The large majority were without electricity, running water, ice, and other essentials we so often take for granted. Some had generators, but fuel supply was very limited. Hot and muggy days brought little relief at night. The missions were extremely hard and sometimes dangerous, but they were also meaningful, loving, fruitful, and fulfilling.

We touched the homes of more than thirty-three families with heavy chainsaw, machinery, and tarp work. We moved everything from limbs, mangled metal, and furniture to huge trees while making egress from homes and removing

Stephen Turner, on a mini excavator, and Rev. Mike Evans talk over next maneuvers as Missouri ERT Leader Scott Burdin drives a skid steer.

trees and debris off homes. Our machinery and its smooth operators made jobs that would have taken days turn into hours.

Our roofing and tarping crews were priority to stop any further damage from rain and such. We use high quality tarps that can last as long as a year. Roofers and carpenters are hard to come by, especially in the aftermath of such a widespread disaster.

Our highest priorities are always the survivors and everyone God put into our paths. This includes other volunteers, emergency workers, community personnel, and people hosting us. The physical task of making their homes safe, sanitary, and secure is important, but our highest priority is always the people God directs us to. We listen to them, cry with them, pray with them, and help them in every way we can. Then we leave them with glimpses of God's love through scripture, prayer, actions, and gestures of pure Christian love.

Every person and family are special to us, but some stand out—such as when the whole town came out to help an elderly blind woman. While we were putting a tarp on her damaged roof, two men came by to put up a new electrical weatherhead, since the old one was destroyed. We assisted them in their task and were able to witness to them and give them scripture cross pens lifting up John 3:16.

An ERT group from Arkansas was assessing damaged homes and getting homeowner's signatures so we could work on them. On the very hot and humid day of September 8, we were sent to one they had assessed at the home of an elderly widow named Clara Russell in Ponchatoula. Her home was mostly intact except for two walls and a rear section of roof that had a huge oak lying on it. We worked relentlessly for three hours, cutting away debris from the electrical weather head so electrical power could possibly be restored, as well as clearing away piles of limbs and debris from her roof. Then we put a 12- by 20-foot tarp over the holes.

After finishing, we were totally exhausted and on our backs in the shade when she drove up.

Above, Rev. Mike Evans hooks a chain to the bucket of an excavator run by Stephen Turner after being wrapped around a big portion of a tree that had crashed through a home. The tree had to be cut up using chainsaws and then lifted out of the home. Below a painting on a storefront in Ponchatoula, Louisiana.

At first she was very angry, walking toward us and shouting, "Who gave y'all permission to work on my home?"

She was thinking we were contractors about to charge her thousands of dollars.

I was on my back with my shoes and socks off and a cool rag over my head on the opposite side of a truck from her, so I somewhat jokingly hollered to Rev. Mike Evans, "Mike, you handle this one!"

Mrs. Russell broke down crying when she found out that we were United Methodists and that all of our work was free. As we gathered for prayer before we left her home, Mrs. Russell started crying again and began lifting praises so loudly to God that her voice rose over Mike's prayer for her and the community.

Many people get taken advantage of by roofers and tree companies looking to make big profits in the aftermath of disasters. We have heard countless stories of where people were charged astronomical prices— from $6,000 to $62,000—to remove trees from their home and property, plus put on tarps. There is nothing wrong with contractors asking a fair price, but price gouging people who are so vulnerable and already hurting so badly after a disaster is simply cruel and totally unethical. When people find out our services and ministry are free, they always immediately give thanks and praise to God.

There were many other such stories from every family we helped, including a woman nicknamed Annie Oakley because she wore a pistol on her side to protect herself and her possessions. One of our teams had the honor and privilege of helping celebrity John Schneider, of *The Dukes of Hazzard* fame, cut up and remove two dangerous trees at his camp that is often used for children's ministries.

We worked side-by-side with other United Methodist ERTs from Louisiana, Missouri, Arkansas, Alabama, Florida, Georgia, Texas, and Mississippi as the Family of God. All together, we were God's church being the church as he has called us to be. Each team shared food, resources, and personnel to accomplish our overall goal of being God's hands and feet to others during such a hurting time.

First United Methodist Church of Ponchatoula did a wonderful job hosting us and accepting us as family. They provided shelter, food, showers, and warm Christian fellowship. Their ministry also reached out to the community as they became a point of distribution for water, ice, flood buckets, tarps, health kits, and other essential items.

ERT volunteer from South Carolina included myself as well as Rev. Mike Evans of Edgefield, Rev. Fred. Buchanan of Orangeburg, Rev. Stephen Turner of

Seneca, Mac and Michael Whitmire of Seneca, Jill Evans of Salem, Curtis Burnett of Greenwood, Worth Adams and Wade Dickens of Florence, David Armstrong of Fort Mill, Hank Edens of Dalzell, and Jerry Pullen of James Island. David Armstrong's brother, Nathan Armstrong, also joined us from Texas.

—Billy Robinson

Throwing Bricks and Breaking Windows

On September 7, 2021, our South Carolina ERT team was in Louisiana in the aftermath of Hurricane Ida.

Before we left for Louisiana, one of our devoted couples, Don and Kathy Beatty, were unable go on the mission. They drove to my home the day before we left and handed me $500 to spend however we needed to. I thanked them and thought we would use it toward fuel or leave it as a gift to the hosting church

After Ida
South Carolina ERTs respond in Christian love after catastrophic Gulf Coast hurricane

At left, Mack Whitmire cuts a huge fallen tree off a shed. At right, the Rev. Mike Evans hooks a chain to an excavator to remove debris. At center, Evans and ERT Coordinator Billy Robinson take a break with John Schneider, of "The Dukes of Hazzard" fame, after their team worked at Schneider's property.

By Billy Robinson and Jessica Brodie

PONCHATOULA, La.—Mangled metal. Newly homeless families. Widespread power and water outages. And in the aftermath, South Carolina stepped up to help.

Hurricane Ida ripped through the northern Gulf Coast Aug. 29, shredding trees and homes and claiming dozens of lives before barreling north with devastating tornadoes and catastrophic flooding. The second most damaging and intense storm in Louisiana history behind Hurricane Katrina, Ida struck on the 16th anniversary of Katrina, bringing maximum sustained winds of 150 mph.

A week later, early disaster response teams deployed from South Carolina to Ponchatoula, Louisiana, and Pass Christian, Mississippi, ultimately assisting with work at 33 homes doing heavy chainsaw, machinery and tarp work.

See "After Ida," Page 24

where we would stay, as we often do.

After dividing into two groups, our team headed to our first assignment in Ponchatoula. Trees were down in the rear of the home, and a big limb with several branches had fallen onto the top of the roof, puncturing two holes in the roof. The limb was still attached to the main trunk twenty plus feet in the air. The homeowner met us and said he had to go to work but stated his insurance requested we not put holes into the roof by nailing down a tarp but to use bricks instead to hold it down. This was a very unusual request, as with a tarp of any big size, you cannot secure it properly without nailing it down. Most times we are putting on tarps to stop further damage to roofs that will later have to be replaced. I looked at the damaged area and saw it would take a small 6x8-foot tarp, so I told him we would do as he asked and use the bricks to secure the tarp.

He left for work, and we got to work, with most of the team on the ground in the backyard while a volunteer from Alabama and I worked from the roof, cutting away the big limb and pulling out the limbs that had protruded into the roof. As we got to a critical point where I had to cut the big limb away from the roof line, I asked Rev. Mike Evans and others on the ground to get one of our ten-foot A-frame ladders and place it in front of one of two large plate glass windows that were unbroken on the rear of the home to protect it in case the limb did not fall as I had planned.

I reached out six to eight feet from the house with a Stihl polesaw and, with a perfected textbook cut, had the limb swing safely away from the home and fall to the ground. It's a maneuver we have performed hundreds of times.

Only, this time it did not simply fall to the ground and lay flat. It fell onto the ground vertically and literally bounced high into the air and backwards into the ladder with such force that it not only broke the plate glass window but also the metal frame around it.

I could not believe it. We pride ourselves on doing good and creating no harm, but today we had destroyed a big window despite our best efforts.

We licked our wounds and continued to work. We got off the roof to grab a tarp. Since it was so small, I told the volunteer from Alabama that he could stay on the ground and I would put it in place. I put the tarp in place and asked Evans to throw some bricks so I could secure the tarp with it. Evans threw up seventeen rather large bricks to me, and I caught each one and put it in place on the tarp. He was throwing from the ground on the side where we had broken the window. But his arm grew tired, so Evans asked the volunteer from Alabama to throw up the last brick. That volunteer was standing on the rear side of the home, where the other unbroken plate glass windows was. He reared back—but instead of throwing it to me, he threw it straight into the plate glass window! It busted to pieces with a loud crash.

I sank to my knees and said, "Lord Jesus, this is our first assignment on this mission that is not starting out very good."

I called the homeowner and asked him to meet us back at his home. When he arrived, I explained the situation to him and handed over the $500 that God had provided us in advance through Don and Kathy. He was fine with the situation, and even hesitant to take the money.

We left him with prayers and scripture resources as we do all survivors. We even joked about people needing pitching lessons and falling limbs that seem to have a mind of their own.

—Billy Robinson

Even Celebrities Need Help

On September 10, 2021, we were finishing up our weeklong disaster response to the Ponchatoula and Pass Christian areas in the aftermath of Hurricane Ida. It was a hard, hot, and humid mission. Our six-person crew headed away from the areas we had been working in to focus on a couple of families in dire need that the Louisiana coordinators wanted us to help, finishing the task around 3:30 p.m. They were having a special supper for us at a church near where we were staying at 6 p.m.

Rev. Mike Evans said to me, "Billy, we are only a couple of miles from where John Schneider has a museum from his days on *The Dukes of Hazzard* TV series. They were some of my childhood heroes. Can we ride by there?"

Several others chimed in, also wanting to go. As we got to the area of the museum, we started seeing a lot of trees down and storm debris. Our hearts dropped as we saw several big trees had fallen into the museum. To top it off, a fire had engulfed much of it. We could see a damaged General Lee car and a car from the movie *Smokey and the Bandit* that was destroyed by fire and a fallen tree.

We started looking around several old wooden buildings that were still standing when Schneider's wife, Alicia, drove up in an early-model station wagon. She invited us to come over to their home, where there was an original General Lee car, and she would call John to meet us there.

We all got excited but none more so than Evans. He got so excited that he got jittery, like a little boy receiving a Christmas gift. We pulled into the driveway of very nice home, and shortly John came driving up in a Kubota side-by-side. He thanked us for coming and helping his state of Louisiana. We took photos and made small talk.

John said he had been cutting up fallen trees and debris since the hurricane at his camp, which he regularly uses as a children's camp. I asked if he needed our help. He replied, "No, I know y'all are busy helping others."

I explained we had just finished for the day and were heading back to South Carolina tomorrow, but that we had time to help now.

He replied, "I do have two big trees that are dangerously leaning over the walking trails and road. If y'all could help me with them, I would sure appreciate it."

As we started toward his camp, John replied, "One of you can ride with me in the side-by-side if you want."

I looked at Mike and said, "Go ahead with John and I will follow."

Mike started grinning from ear to ear, then sprang out of the truck like a deer and into John's side-by-side, sitting right next to John.

Rev. Mike Evans, Dukes of Hazzard star John Schneider, and Billy Robinson take a break after cutting up two big, dangerous trees at Schneider's property and camp for children.

We got to the camp and saw that John and a few others had been doing a lot of clean up since the hurricane. There was a big limb practically broken ten feet off the ground and dangerously hanging over a walking trail next to a pond.

I took lead on it as Mike—in hog heaven—rode off with John to another dangerous tree.

It took some serious thought-processing and carefully developed plans, but within two hours, we had the trees cut down and hauled off by John on his tractor.

We then focused on literally getting a tree out of a pond. This required us cutting all the limbs away that we could reach and Mike riding on the bucket of John's tractor (with John driving) into the water and tying a rope around the tree trunk. John pulled it out, and we all cut it up, including John with his chainsaw.

This was a unique ending to a very wild and intense mission. We found John Schneider to be a down-to-earth, hard-working man who loved people and made us feel like family. He was able to open his camp back up for visitors coming the following weekend.

John invited us to join him at a fundraiser concert for hurricane victims the next night along with several other musicians. We had to decline, as we were heading back to South Carolina with the rest of the team the next morning.

But looking back on it, Mike and I and any others who wanted to should have stayed one more day.

—Billy Robinson

Chapter 45

Winter Storm Izzy Provides an Honor and a Joy
January 17, 2022

South Carolina United Methodist Volunteers in Mission Early Response Teams had a strong and quick response after Winter Storm Izzy, with fourteen sets of boots on the ground within twenty-four hours of the icy wintry mix that caused trees to crash into homes in Greenwood on January 16, 2022.

The January 17 mission was coordinated in conjunction with the Greenwood County emergency services director by Rev. Mike Evans, the United Methodist Greenwood District disaster coordinator. Volunteers braved the icy cold conditions that created wind chill in the twenties accompanied by thirty-mile-per-hour arctic winds. We were honored to have then-Greenwood District Superintendent Dr. Stephen Love work alongside up us for the day.

The conditions made it extremely hard to tarp roofs after removing the fallen trees and ice-covered debris.

Evans coordinated with city officials and other volunteers to make sure one homeowner, Jane Copeland of Logan Drive, had space heaters and the means to heat her water since the fallen tree had destroyed her heating and air unit and gas connection.

This wonderful lady was so appreciative of the acts of genuine love, care, and concern she received. She told Evans, "I did not know that we United Methodists had this wonderful ministry!" Oh, what an honor and joy it is, with blessing beyond all measure, to be a part of God's hands and feet to people during their times of need.

Responders from the Greenwood District were Evans and Dr. Love as well as Greenwood District Lay Servant Ministries Director Cathy Trevino, Dawn

Elaine Turner and Felix Vazquez carry off a log with ice on it after Winter Storm Izzy.

Rhodes, Bill and Elaine Turner, Curtis Burnett, Tony Watson, Sandy Shafer, and Leonard May. Other responders were Jerry Pullen from James Island and Felix Vazquez, Michael Hughes, and myself from North.

—*Billy Robinson*

Chapter 46

Working Hard with Smiling Faces and Positive Attitudes
April 7-8, 2022

On the afternoon of Tuesday, April 5, 2022, strong thunderstorms and multiple tornadoes ravaged parts of South Carolina. One of the tornadoes was an EF3 for most of its thirty-nine-mile path from Ulmer to Bowman. At its widest portion it was 500 yards wide. The weather service said it had the power of an EF4 when it touched down in a pine tree plantation, snapping all the big trees five feet off the ground and decimating the forest.

Thankfully the tornado happened in a rural area and was constantly touching down and picking up off the ground throughout its path, or the damage would have been much worse.

When it touched down just outside of Branchville on Freedom Road, however, it was an EF3 and damaged thirteen homes in the community. By the grace of God, no one was seriously injured, though many big trees were violently thrown to the ground, the majority of them falling across driveways and near homes. A few trees fell onto some homes, causing roof damage and breaking windows.

The following day, more violent storms rocked our state, hindering aid to the affected areas. Orangeburg County Emergency Services Director Billy Staley contacted our South Carolina United Methodist Volunteers in Mission Early Response Teams on Wednesday night, asking us to aid the families affected.

The next morning, Thursday, we responded first with assessment teams, who contacted the survivors and assessed their needs, prayed for them, and offered scripture aids of comfort and care.

Then Friday, April 8, through late Saturday, ERT teams responded with twen-

Bryan Williams of North cuts a big pine tree away from the side and roofline of a home.

ty-one volunteers from the state, as well as two disaster response trailers and two skid steers to take on the phenomenal task of cutting up the big trees with chainsaws at eleven homes. Teams also piled the debris in wood lines since the county was not going to pick up the storm debris. We also tarped seven homes and structures with damaged roofs and windows to prevent further weather damage.

We started by cutting a big pine tree away from the side and roofline of a home and placed tarps over three broken windows for a grateful family unable to do the task themselves because of health issues. We followed suit from house to house in the vicinity and across the road, saving homeowners tens of thousands of dollars and making their homes accessible and livable again. In several locations, we also cut out access so the power company could restore power to the homes.

On Seacrest Lane, we found family helping family, some traveling from Charleston to do so. We worked side by side with them, cutting fallen trees and debris away and tarping damaged roofs.

The last home we worked at was a unique one, where a big oak tree had fallen over and into Bob and Diane Williams's shed. The tree was completely covering the shed, making access to it impossible and dangerous because of the building's partial collapse.

Using a skid steer and chainsaws, we methodically and carefully removed the big tree from the shed. We were then able to save most of the shed's contents, including a collection of more than 300 elephant collectibles, educational items for kids, and various other items. The salvaged items were loaded onto a trailer and hauled to their home. A tarp was placed over the severely damaged shed to help salvage half of it and protect its remaining contents.

The homeowners kept saying they were so grateful and had never witnessed or even heard of a group of people who would come out in the midst of a disaster to voluntarily help complete strangers in need.

Mr. Williams teared up as he stated, "Y'all work so hard and somehow keep a smile on your face at all times."

I replied, "We are so blessed and find great joy, hope, fulfillment, excitement, and much love in being God's hands and feet to others in need. It is truly our honor and privilege to represent the love of Jesus in such caring ways. We become so much better people and are so blessed ourselves when we heed God's calling to be our brother and sister's keeper. We are the church being the church as Jesus Christ calls us to be! Anything less would be unacceptable."

—*Billy Robinson*

Chapter 47

Rescuing a Community Center with a Surgeon's Touch
July 9, 2022

On July 9, 2022, South Carolina United Methodist Volunteers in Mission Early Response Teams responded to the Camden area, where a recent storm had left a damaged tree on a community center that was recently the Baron DeKalb Elementary School.

Rev. Fred Buchanan cuts down the remaining portion of a tree as an ERT volunteer chain uses a rope to pull the standing tree away from the former Baron DeKalb Elementary School, now a community center. Pulling from front are Ben Tobin, Michael Hughes, Felix Vazquez, Rev. James Smith, and Don Gearhard.

Three other trees also presented a danger to the facility and needed to be cut down. In addition, there were three pine trees laying across a fence line in the rear of the property. The eight-person ERT crew was made up of volunteers from within a 200-mile range.

The project was headed up by Rev. James Smith and others, including his wife, Rev. Millie Nelson Smith, director of Connectional Ministries for the South Carolina Conference of The United Methodist Church. The Smiths are in the process of repurposing the school as a community and outreach center.

The ERT team began by using a winch and chainsaws to pull away the big tree that was dangerously resting on an array of windows and the side and top of the facility. Extreme caution had to be taken to prevent further damage.

With a surgeon's precision, the damaged tree was removed, and the facility was spared any further damage. Three other trees posing a future danger were also taken down and the fence line cleared of downed trees and temporally repaired.

Hot temperatures and physically exhausting conditions could not hamper the God-inspired enthusiasm and willingness to complete the mission so the facility can be used for a wide variety of future missions.

—Billy Robinson

Chapter 48

Meticulous Ingenuity
August 10, 2022

On August 10, a South Carolina United Methodist Volunteers in Mission Early Response Team responded to the home of Carl Strock in Cope, South Carolina, after a recent storm felled a huge post oak tree. A seven-person team comprising three ERT volunteers and three others from St. Paul United Methodist Church were led by Rev. Fred Buchanan of St. Paul UMC, Orangeburg. The tree was blocking an access road to the home of Strock, a member of St. Paul UMC.

St. Paul UMC members take on the monumental task of cutting a big post oak out of a driveway near Orangeburg. From left, Ken Stovell looks on as Dr. Gene Atkinson and Rev. Fred Buchanan cut with chainsaws.

The team came equipped with big chainsaws to take on the huge oak. The oak was meticulously resting over and partially on a special mailbox and hay rake, so the team had to use a lot of ingenuity to get the equipment out without further damaging them. A very hot and humid day added to the exhausting task.

But within four hours, the task was completed and the driveway cleared.

Team members included myself along with Buchanan and Strock, Dr. Gene Atkinson, Ken Stovell, Jim Cary, and Felix Vazquez.

—Billy Robinson

Chapter 49

Perfect Storm, Deadly Crisis
August 22-26, 2022

South Carolina's United Methodist Volunteers in Mission Early Response Team responded to a plea for help from Kentucky after deadly and devastating flooding there. From July 28 through the first part of August, large amounts of heavy rain fell, as much as eleven inches in some areas in a day's time.

This created what some would call a "perfect storm" of adverse conditions, leading to a deadly crisis in Eastern Kentucky. Flash flooding caused rivers and creeks to turn into torrents of violent raging water that decimated everything in their path, claiming vehicles, homes, animals, and at least thirty-nine lives.

To make matters worse, this area contains some of the poorest counties in the United States. What little some people had was literally swept away, and they have no means of replacing homes, clothes, and transportation.

Our team of twenty-one volunteers were led by Rev. Mike Evans and Chuck Marshall. We came with big, caring, and loving hearts along with two ERT trailers filled with disaster relief work tools and supplies.

This was the first response for ERT Trailer SC-10, which was one of three new trailers recently completed and stocked. The trailer was purchased through donations from volunteers across the South Carolina Conference of The United Methodist Church.

We were sent to Jackson, Kentucky, and stayed at Hampton United Methodist Church, which was a wonderful host.

Jill Evans of our team headed up our base camp operations.

Our trip included a mission within a mission, as Lamar UMC in Lamar,

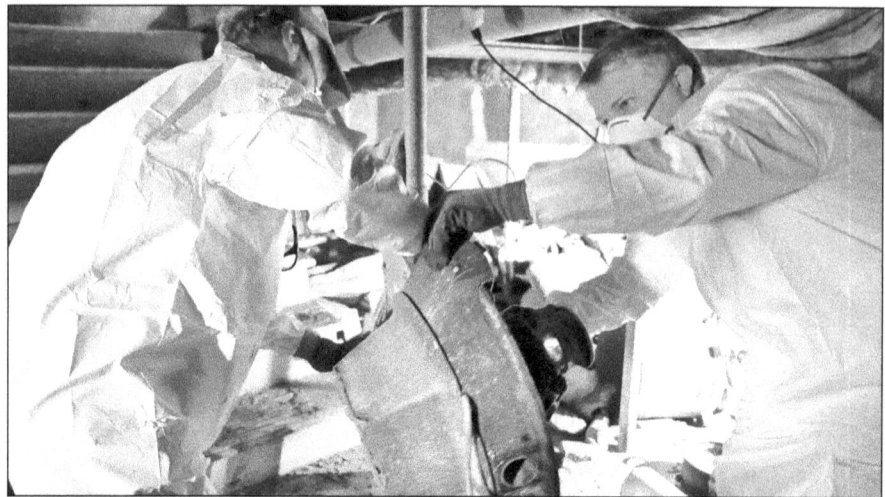

Crews muck out a flooded basement filled with mud, muck, and mold.

South Carolina, contacted our conference office to tell about a very successful ministry of theirs led by Marilyn Lawhon and backed by Rev. Paula Stover, in which many supplies for Kentucky were collected by their church.

Before we headed to Kentucky, we picked up a U-Haul trailer in Florence loaded with a wide variety of needed essential supplies from Lamar UMC. We offloaded the vital supplies at the Methodist Mountain Mission in Jackson, Kentucky, to a very grateful mission group who were striving hard meet the needs of so many devastated people.

In Jackson, our disaster response teams were first directed to the downtown area of Sycamore Street, where water had flooded the police station and other county offices. Many homes were affected, with floodwaters that averaged five feet into the homes, destroying all their furniture and possessions. The people were all racing the clock, trying to muck out and clean out their homes before mold and hazardous conditions took over to the extent that they would have to be destroyed.

Susan Spencer told about how she went door to door on the worst night of the flooding telling her neighbors to evacuate. Two of her neighbors were in their eighties and refused to leave their homes, stating the waters had never risen that high before. In 1984 and 2021, water did come up onto the street, but only into the floor of a few homes near the creek that was forty feet below them in a ravine. They knew it would take a phenomenal amount of water to rise into their homes.

Susan kept at the elderly homeowners until they finally submitted and left their homes with family persuasion. Susan's actions, and the actions of other

The team included, kneeling from left, Chuck Knight, Jill Evans, Tony Watson, Elaine Turner, Rev. Scott Bratton, Billy Robinson, and Dr. John Gemmell, and standing from left, Mary Watson, Curtis Burnett, Hank Edens, Rev. Mike and Heather Evans, Phil Griswold, Mike Luther, Dawn Rhodes, Jerry Pullen, Dan Dowbridge, Worth Adams, Chuck Marshall, Bill Turner, and Mark Honeg.

people like her, saved many lives that night as the waters swiftly rose and engulfed homes.

A friend of Susan's named Patricia Baker came to visit and help as needed while we were there. Patricia told about her horrific story on the worst night of flooding. Her husband had died a couple years prior, so she was at home by herself. She became extremely concerned and then frightened as she watched the flood rapidly overtake her home in the dark of night. Adding to her level of terror was the fact that she could not swim.

As her home was swept away from its foundation, Patricia found herself thrown from the home into raging floodwaters, fighting for her life. She was able to grab hold of the back bumper of her husband's car and held on as it was also swept away into the wildly raging torrent of water.

The car hit a tree, which threw her off onto the tree. She grabbed hold of the tree in the dark and literally held on for dear life until morning, when a National Guard Helicopter rescued her out of the tree.

One of Patricia's cousins and several neighbors died, and her whole world was turned upside down. She lost everything she owned. Yet there she was, out trying to help others in need despite her horrific experience.

We split into two and sometimes three teams, mucking and cleaning out the flooded homes. This encompassed tearing out waterlogged Sheetrock, flooring, and fixtures. We worked with passion to show the love of Jesus Christ to so many hurting people while also getting all the good work done possible while we were there.

The hot and humid temperatures beat down on all of us, but with God's strength and determination, we were able to persevere.

Complicating the strenuous work was one of our worst enemies—mold. This forced us to take extra protective measures, such as wearing masks, respirators, and Tyvek suits. We had to constantly monitor each other to make sure we did not get any heat-related injuries. We also sprayed the homes to kill the mold.

One home we worked on was for Cynthia Bell, who is a physician's assistant. Cynthia had recently finished her training and was offered jobs in more prominent areas, but she chose to return to a poorer county where she could be most effective in helping people. We were honored to remove all the flood-damaged materials from her home.

Next door, at the home of Austin Craft, the family had been mucking out their home one day at a time without any professional help. All members had allergies and two had asthma. The active mold spores had them on antibiotics, yet they were determined to get back into their home and were doing all they could to make it happen. They said they were at their wit's end when God showed up through us and took over.

It was a daunting task. In the center of their home was a huge basement with no outside access. The basement had filled with water, mud, and muck during the flooding and had not been touched. Most of the water had gradually seeped out of a drain, leaving wet, muddy residue everywhere. Active mold was on the rafters and throughout, along with the stench and hazards left by the flooding aftermath. The slippery muddy and hot conditions made the task much more difficult, along with the fact that we had to bring everything up a narrow set of stairs through the interior of the house to the roadside.

According to locals, there were more than 800 suspension footbridges in the path of destruction. The floods destroyed all but a few. This cut off a lot of people's access to their homes and property.

Chuck Marshall led one of our teams to help shore up one of these bridges for the family of Tim Gilbert. (See related story in this chapter.) The bridge was still standing but needed shoring for stability and a handrail added. Tim's wife had been transported to a local hospital for medical issues the night before our arrival. EMS had to hand-carry her through the waist-deep creek in the dark to get her to an awaiting ambulance. Our team was able to stabilize the bridge

Elaine Turner carries out water- and mold-damaged Sheetrock from a home in Jackson, Kentucky.

and added handrails to make it safe. As our team was leaving the job site, Mrs. Gilbert crossed the bridge for the first time in three weeks to get her mail out of the mailbox.

We are so thankful for the honor and privilege to represent Jesus to so many people in need. The physical labor was only one aspect. Listening to and caring about the survivors and all others, including emergency response personnel and team members, is where the real healing begins, and where all (including us) receive the most fulfillment.

We shared Jesus's love through scripture and care goods, plus handshakes, hugs, sweat, tears, minor injuries, and sore muscles, all while tolerating dirty and filthy conditions. We overcame fears of mold, COVID, major injuries, vehicle wrecks, financial situations, and a wide variety of concerns. We were so blessed by our conference and home churches that we were able to cover everyone's expenses and leave $2,000 in additional donations to the local United Methodist churches there to disperse as needed.

We worked on seven homes and repaired one footbridge, putting in 580 volunteer hours. To God be the glory.

Volunteers included myself along with Rev. Mike and Heather Evans, Chuck Marshall, Jill Evans, Dawn Rhodes, Curtis Burnett, Bill and Elaine Turner, Mike

Luther, Phil Griswold, Worth Adams, Rev. Scott Bratton, Dr. John Gemmell, Tony and Mary Watson, Hank Edens, Mark Honeg, Jerry Pullen, Chuck Knight, and Dan Dowbridge.

—Billy Robinson

A Fruitful Mountain Detour

On August 22, 2022, South Carolina ERTs were called to Jackson, Kentucky, to assist residents following a severe flood. We had around twenty certified ERTs, as well as three disaster trailers from Greenwood, Orangeburg, and Spartanburg. The call-out was led by Rev. Mike Evans from Greenwood, Billy Robinson from Orangeburg, and me.

While we stayed busy working on as many as five houses a day, one call for help kept drawing our attention. The address was about an hour away. It was not easy to get to because of its location at the top of a mountain pass. The owner said there was nowhere to park vehicles and trailers since the road was so narrow.

We were drawn to the fact that he and his wife were in poor health and lived in a house that was across a creek. You had to cross a narrow footbridge to get to the house. These footbridges are quite common in this area of Kentucky. During the flooding, the footbridge had washed down the creek, leaving them with no way to get to the parking area, which was across the bridge and next to the road. Several nights prior to this, his wife had experienced a medical emergency, and the paramedics had to carry her across the creek in knee-deep water in an ambulance cot to get to the road and the waiting emergency vehicles.

We kept putting this request off because of the distance to drive and the fact that we had a stack of other requests right there in the town of Jackson. But for some reason, this request kept coming back to us. After consulting with Mike and Billy, I called Tim Gilbert, the homeowner, and spoke with him about his needs. He told me he understood there was so much need in the town and we probably couldn't reach the address pulling a trailer, since there was nowhere to park or turn the trailer around.

Well, don't tell a team of ERTs they can't get a storm victim's needs met and expect them to let it go. With Mike and Billy's support, we loaded up the Spartanburg ERT trailer and about seven ERTs. We left Jackson and drove up through the mountains. We drove past washed-out roads, school buses washed into the creeks, and house trailers on their sides. Finally we reached the address

During the flooding, one couple's footbridge had washed down the creek, leaving them with no way to get to their parking area, which was across the bridge and next to the road.

at the top of the mountain. It had a small turn-off area next to the creek, and the house was on the far side of the creek. We located the old footbridge, which had washed downstream about 200 feet and was embedded in brush and debris.

We began working as soon as we arrived and introduced ourselves to the resident. Together, we had an opening prayer and formed a plan. We retrieved the old bridge and located enough large rocks and cinderblocks to stabilize it where it had originally been. Mr. Gilbert asked if we could build a handrail onto the bridge since his wife was in very poor health and was not stable enough to walk over the bridge and to the car without a rail. It was way too far to go back out to Jackson and bring back construction material, so we decided to "go old school" and cut some large limbs from the nearby woods. We formed them into straight rails and made a custom, although primitive, handrail for the bridge. We also cut some logs from the woods and reinforced the underside of the bridge to limit the sway when someone was walking on it. I have to say, after almost twenty years of disaster recovery work, this was the first time we had been asked to rebuild a bridge.

As we got the trailer turned around to leave—no easy matter—we saw his wife had crossed the bridge for the first time in two weeks so she could check the mailbox. Suddenly, all the effort to get there was well worth it.

It was time to go back to Jackson and start another job.

ERTs who assisted included Mike Luther, John Gemmell, Dan Dowbridge, Phil Griswold, Hank Edens, Mark Honeg, and me.

—Chuck Marshall

Kentucky ERT Experience

There are numerous events I could tell you about our trip to flood-torn Jackson, Kentucky. Most deal with loss but thankfulness that God has seen them through.

There is one particular account that stands out as a true example that God is our ever-present help in trouble. The lady's name is Brenda. She gave me a pretty detailed life sketch, and suffice it to say that Brenda has not had an easy life. Things in her life were indeed improving. She and her fiancé had purchased a house at a very good price. Drug addicts had lived there before them and had pretty much trashed the place. With hard work, Brenda and her family were making the house livable.

Then the flood came.

The day it happened, several neighbors had come by and told her she needed to leave. She ignored their concerns as there was no water on the street in front of her house. The last time someone came by to tell her to leave, she noticed water was covering the street. She gathered a few things for each person living there. By the time she got those things together, the water was up the steps of her house and starting to come in the door.

You must realize her house was several hundred yards from the creek, which sat at least fifty feet below that area. By the time Brenda left, she was wading through waist-deep water.

After the flood that rose five feet in her home, Brenda and six other family members were given a one-bedroom apartment to stay in thirty miles from Jackson. Her fiancé and several people were able to get all the walls back to the studs. She said her fellow church members would have helped, but they were helping their preacher, whose house had been flooded along with the church building.

Brenda learned that her family had seven days before they would have to leave the apartment. She knew the flooring had to be removed and had been told a crew would come in and put up Sheetrock and subflooring if she could get the house ready. However, her fiancé had to work. She worked from home and was pregnant, yet she was not supposed to be in the house because of mold. Brenda grew desperate.

Our South Carolina ERT team was in Jackson on Monday afternoon looking at the houses where we had been scheduled to work. We were in our bright green ERT shirts. Our team leader, Chuck Marshall, happened to be standing in the street right in front of Brenda's house.

Brenda was on the porch and had just pleaded with God that she needed help. Then she turned and saw a guy in a green shirt standing there. She said something told her to go talk to him, that he would help.

Well, the rest of the story is pretty simple. Chuck and Rev. Mike Evans agreed we needed to help. They added Brenda's house to the workload. On Tuesday, a team went in and removed the hardwood flooring and the subflooring, getting down to the joists. In a day and a half, they were done.

Brenda was there every morning. Brenda knew who the "something" was that told her to ask Chuck for help. Brenda knew God had indeed answered her plea.

—*Mary Watson*

Chapter 50

God's Provision During Hurricane Ian
October 1, 2022

South Carolina United Methodist Volunteers in Mission Early Response Teams worked hard in the aftermath of Hurricane Ian, which made landfall in South Carolina on September 30, 2022, causing heavy rainfall, storm surge, downed trees, power outages, and more.

Twenty-five ERT volunteers put in 252 volunteer hours using ERT trailers, tractors, chainsaws, and tarps, plus pumped out a church basement. In addition, volunteers gave out flood buckets at Little River United Methodist Church, Little River, and St. Paul's Waccamaw UMC, Pawleys Island, October 1, 2020.

We placed tarps on three homes and worked at ten sites doing chainsaw and debris removal. We used sump pumps to pump out a flooded basement at Holly Hill UMC, plus provided four homes with individual tarps to cover their belongings.

Volunteers responded in Holly Hill, Vance, Charleston, North Charleston, Summerville, and McClellanville. Two tarps were handed out in Florence and one in Marion. Chuck Marshall coordinated the work and responses through Crisis Cleanup.

—Billy Robinson

Chapter 51

A God-Sized Challenge in McClellanville
OCTOBER 7, 2022

On October 7, 2022, a five-person South Carolina United Methodist Volunteers in Mission Early Response Team responded to a special follow-up call to the home of Zedra Flowers near McClellanville.

After Hurricane Ian, the homeowner faced a unique and precarious situation as a huge pecan tree had split, and its stump was partially attached to very large portion of it and was perched two feet over the family's water pump. It was only a matter of time before it fell, further crushing the family's water pump and water tank.

The large family had several small children, and when this happened, they would be out of water, plus face hefty costs to get it repaired and have the tree removed. Several other volunteer organizations had looked at the situation and walked away, saying it was too risky.

We accepted the God-sized challenge just as we had in countless other situations throughout the Southeast since 2005. After all, we serve a miracle-working God.

A couple of us looked at the job a few days prior while doing other ERT work nearby. We prayed hard over the decision to help, as if we crushed the tank and pump then we would be obligated to pay for a new one out of our personal funds.

However, we all felt God's call to help this family out of this bad situation.

With God's direction and our faith in him, we meticulously started cutting away at the tree and placed logs, a fifty-five-gallon drum, and old tires around the

Hurricane Ian caused heavy rainfall, storm surge, downed trees, power outages, and more across the state.

tank and water pump to protect them the best we could.

Then came the moment of truth as Jerry Harris controlled the bucket of his tractor beneath the big tree, with Don Beatty's truck hooked to the tree with a rope to pull it away, when Jerry picked up and pushed forward. We all looked to God with one last prayer.

As I coordinated the attack plan of pushing and pulling, God miraculously took things into his hands again, as he has done so many times in the past. The God-given plan worked to perfection, and the tree was laid to the side of the tank and pump with precision.

We lifted our hands high and cheered, "Praise the Lord!"

Then we finished cutting up the fallen tree and moving the debris to a pile.

Responders were Don and Kathy Beatty, Jerry Harris, Michael Hughes, and me.

—*Billy Robinson*

Chapter 52

Shining the Light of Jesus into the Darkness
NOVEMBER 6-13 AND 13-18, 2022

South Carolina United Methodist Volunteers in Mission Early Response Teams responded to Fort Myers, Florida, in the aftermath of Hurricane Ian. The Category 4 hurricane, which made landfall there September 28, decimated portions of that area with 155 mile per hour winds and waves of floodwaters. Its deadly destructive path tore across Florida and made it the deadliest hurricane to strike that state since the 1935 Labor Day Hurricane.

Infrastructure in the affected areas of Florida was so impacted that it took more than a month before United Methodist Disaster Response was able to receive and sustain out-of-state ERTs. In the meantime, we in South Carolina responded to hurricane's impact in our state, making ERT responses from Charleston to Florence, with Charleston and McClellanville receiving the main portions of ERT-requested help.

Team Alpha

On November 6-13, 2022, South Carolina ERT Team Alpha responded to the Fort Myers area, staying at Faith United Methodist Church with twenty-eight volunteers, three ERT disaster response trailers and two skid steers. We brought with us flood buckets and a variety of supplies and donations for the survivors and church.

We were directed to the worst-hit areas, focusing our efforts mainly on muck out and clean out of flooded homes that received as much as seven feet of salt water throughout. We also placed tarps on the damaged roofs of three homes, did some chainsaw work, and used the skid steer to move debris.

Frank Gramling, Matthew Brautigam, Josh Riddle, Steve Bishop, and Dan Dowbridge tote a soaked and molded couch out of a flooded home in Fort Myers, Florida.

Up and down most streets we could see massive piles of debris that contained the physical remnants of many homes and lives, including waterlogged photos and precious treasured items destroyed by water and mold.

Mold was a major concern, and we took all needed precautions for our personal safety and that of the survivors who worked alongside us in several locations.

One flooded home that we worked on was the home of Pete Crumpacker, located three blocks from the ocean. His home had sustained six-and-a-half feet of salt water, and no help had been received since the hurricane. The home was filled with his family's possessions plus furniture and appliances. Mold covered everything from the floor to the ceiling.

Pete, like so many others, had no flood insurance because of the high cost of obtaining it. He had lost a lot. What could be salvaged, including the structure of his home, was in dire jeopardy because of mold and associated hazards. He needed get everything out and sprayed soon.

Pete kept flooding us with appreciation for our willingness to help with such a dirty and hazardous undertaking, to which we gave all the glory to God. He began to tell how his wife was so overwhelmed with emotion and sorrow that she could not even go back to their home. She was very depressed and had a hard time dealing with the entire disaster, which literally almost took her and Pete's life.

They had decided to ride out the hurricane, which was almost a fatal mistake. Pete told that as the floodwaters rose in the dark of night, they began to climb

Jerry Pullen, Matthew Brautigam, and Josh Riddle move a clothes dryer out of a flooded home in Fort Myers as Don Beatty looks on.

onto furniture and then the countertops to stay out of the water. As the floodwaters continued to rise, the refrigerator began to float, and they eventually had to climb onto it to survive. Pete took a hatchet and chopped a hole into the attic so they could keep their heads above the water. As he was chopping a hole into the roof, the water began to subside, and their lives were spared.

Pete had such a wonderful attitude and was always smiling. We commented about his wonderful disposition, and he stated, "I am so thankful to Jesus for sparing our lives and realize that the rest is just material things. When life gives you a lemon, make lemonade."

Team leader Rev. Mike Evans tells about a man named Walter Graham, who his team was sent to help.

As Evans said, "Walter was flooded out and in dire straits. A company had charged him $8,000 to remove the furniture out of his home and did not include removing all the cabinets, paneling, Sheetrock, insulation, etc., or mucking it out, which is what we did. Walter started crying tears of joy when he found out our services were free. Walter talked of how our ERTs gave him renewed hope amid a seemingly hopeless situation. He kept thanking everyone, and we once again directed all the praise and glory to God, who equips us, sustains us, and is our Lord and redeemer."

The Category 1 Hurricane Nicole caused us to leave a day earlier than expected and drive through stormy weather.

Mounds of debris piles were stacked near the ocean in Fort Myers, Florida.

Team Bravo

South Carolina ERT Team Bravo responded from November 13-18 with seventeen volunteers, two ERT trailers and one skid steer.

Their first stop was at Pete's house to tear out around two bathrooms and then on to five other muck out and clean out jobs at homes, as well as some skid steer work and tarping of homes.

Team leader Chuck Marshall said the people were so devastated and down, in a depressed state.

"We are so thankful to shine the light of Jesus into their areas of darkness and bring God's hope and love to them," Marshall said. "Our teams are working so hard and diligent, and I am so proud of them."

Team leader Rev. Stephen Turner added, "Just because it is not still in the mainstream news does not mean that everything is back to normal. Far from it, for years to come. We need to continue to pray and support the people until it is."

We were blessed this past year with three new heavy-duty ERT trailers and additional ERT equipment from generous donations from across our conference, making this long-distance mission possible.

—Billy Robinson

Lessons from Duct Tape

In November 2022, I decided to go on my first ERT trip. We went to Fort Myers, Florida. I did not know what to expect because I had never seen any hurricane damage before in person, only on TV. And let me say the TV doesn't do it justice.

We arrived in Florida at the church that was hosting us. I got settled in, and contacts were made with families that needed help. Decisions were made about which homes we would try to help.

The next day, we went out and helped a family whose house needed to be mucked out. Yuck! On the third day we went to another home that needed to be tarped. I chose to get on the roof and help. The winds were blowing up to forty miles per hour, which made it even more "fun."

As I was sliding across the roof to pull the tarp and help nail—yes, I said "help nail" (scary)—someone pointed out that I had a hole in my pants. I had caught my pants on some protruding nails and tore a big hole in my pants!

We continued to tarp the roof, and when we were finished, I went down and a friend put a piece of duct tape over the hole in my pants.

Moral of the story: You know you're a redneck when you fix holes in your clothes with duct-tape.

—*Tina F. Knight*

Chapter 53

Finding Hope and Comfort Amid a Pile of Rubble
April 9-13, 2023

On March 25, 2023, a deadly outbreak of tornadoes struck Mississippi, leaving a trail of destruction thru Mississippi and Alabama. Twenty-five people in Mississippi were killed with massive destruction throughout the communities of Silver City, Rolling Fork, and surrounding areas.

The call for help from South Carolina United Methodist Volunteers in Mission's Early Response Team came on Easter Sunday, April 9, to send teams.

When we arrived at the sponsoring church in Winona, Mississippi, we were asked to help in a lesser-known area of the county called Black Hawk that had received very little support.

The team arrived at a homesite where there once was a modular home but now only had a concrete slab with broken tiedowns, two cars covered in debris, and all the family's belongings scattered through the woods.

It was obvious this was a family that loved and cared for the property. The grounds were meticulously groomed beneath the destruction. Children's toys, playground equipment, and bikes were strewn about the property. The disaster coordinator for the United Methodist response informed us that the mother, father, and one twin son were killed in the tornado. One fourteen-year-old boy survived but was thrown into a nearby cow pasture. He was mostly unharmed physically but emotionally devastated.

Our team leader spoke with the grieving family and asked what we could do to help them. Usually ERT work involves removal of tree debris, tarping roofs, or cleaning out damaged homes, but none of that was needed at this site. The

In March 2023, a deadly outbreak of tornadoes struck Mississippi, leaving a trail of destruction thru Mississippi and Alabama.

family was emotionally unable to return to the site since the tornado destroyed it.

The older son asked if he could help them find some important papers, keys, and perhaps save anything salvageable for them as they simply could not face it all.

As the team worked through the debris field, we were able to find items the family needed. We kept in touch with them as we collected the salvaged items. The neighbors were amazed that we were willing to do this for their community. Many of them commented that no one had been there to help.

The oldest son came by to thank us and was amazed at how much we had been able to do in one day. His fourteen-year-old brother was not dealing with the loss well, and he thought it would be good for him to come back to the site while we were there.

On the second day, the boy arrived along with many of the extended family. We were able to minister to this entire family through God's love and grace.

While this was not the usual ERT call out, God sent us to this place to help a family who had lost hope. You never know how God will use you, but if you have a willing heart, he will guide you.

—*Kathy Beatty*

Chapter 54

God's Grace, Mercy, and Renewed Hope in Valdosta
September 4-14, 2023

Two South Carolina United Methodist Volunteers in Mission Early Response Teams comprising twenty-nine volunteers responded to South Georgia in the aftermath of Hurricane Idalia over a two-week period from September 4-14, 2023.

By then a Category 2 storm, torrential rains from the hurricane caused widespread flooding, uprooted trees, and destroyed buildings in Valdosta, Georgia, prompting a call for assistance from South Georgia United Methodist Conference's Disaster Response Team.

Immediately, South Carolina's ERT got to work mobilizing a team to help.

Billy Robinson, South Carolina ERT coordinator, and Rev. Mike Evans assembled a crew of eighteen men and women hailing from Charleston to Honea Path, calling them Team Alpha. Two disaster response trailers and a tractor accompanied the team.

Team Alpha traveled to Valdosta September 4-9, staying at Camp Tygart near Ray City, Georgia. The energetic team spent long days helping people in need in the name of Jesus, doing a lot of massive chainsaw work, some tarp work on storm-damaged roofs, and much clearing of debris. We met a lot of interesting people full of character and excited about life and living, especially since their lives had been spared.

One elderly man dressed in a cowboy outfit, including boots and a hat, kept visiting us at his sister's yard that had numerous big trees down. He kept thanking us for coming to their aid, offering us water, and adding a lot of joy to our day.

Crews were able to stand one fallen tree back up for a homeowner. They dubbed the up-righted tree "The Bishop's Tree" because of the connection between the homeowner and the South Carolina Conference.

We had several skid steers and tractors with our team, and we divided them to help make our teams safer and more efficient. The Whitmire family from Tamassee, South Carolina, has put in a lot of hard work over the past couple of years tackling some difficult jobs. This trip was no exception as they turned disaster sites into clean yards clear of debris, making survivors' lives into a better "new normal" and giving them renewed hope.

A handicapped lady named Darlene Ray, who lives alone near Valdosta, saw one of our South Carolina disaster trailers in transit to a disaster site. She was desperate for help, so she googled South Carolina Volunteers in Missions and called our conference office. The call was directed to Tammy Fulmer.

Fulmer called Robinson and Evans, who were hard at work in a devastated debris field of several downed trees encompassing three homes, and told them about Darlene's need and her call for help. That afternoon, South Carolina ERT responded to Darlene, who had a hard time getting into her home with a blown-down tree blocking some access to her home and four trees down in her yard. She needed a lot of help, and by God's grace and mercy, Evans's team was able to come to her aid, including standing back up one smaller tree that meant so much to her, as her mother had planted it years ago. Evans' team accomplished the task and decided to call the up-righted tree "The Bishop's Tree" because of the connection between Darlene and our South Carolina Conference.

Team Bravo was led by Chuck Marshall and Stephen Turner in Valdosta for the week of September 10-14 with eleven volunteers, one disaster trailer, and two

Above, Steve Bishop of Charleston cuts out big chunks of debris from a fallen oak that crashed into a home near Valdosta, Georgia. Below, ERT members Rev. Mike Evans, left, and Billy Robinson, right, share a smile with a Valdosta resident who survived the storm.

skid steers. They performed a lot of hard work at fourteen homes.

Both teams focused on hard work to help those in dire need but mainly prioritized meeting the survivors' spiritual and emotional needs along with emergency responders and coordinators in the affected areas. This includes much Christian love in the forms of prayer, listening to the survivors, meeting their basic needs, offering comfort, and distributing Christian resources

While South Carolina's damage from Idalia was relatively minor, ERT members also pitched in to help in Holly Hill, where a huge oak tree crashed to the ground in front of Holly Hill United Methodist Church, blocking some access to the church and the roadway.

Rev. John Elmore, a few other ERT members, and Billy Robinson worked together to cut the tree away and got word out that help was available if anyone needed it.

—Jessica Brodie and Billy Robinson

Chapter 55

Daunting, Dangerous, and Unique Situations
January 9, 2024

On the evening of January 9, Rev. Mike Evans led a combination team of South Carolina United Methodist Volunteers in Mission Early Response Team volunteers and Edgefield volunteer firefighters to cut a tree away and off a home, plus tarp damaged portions at a home on Circle Street in Edgefield.

On January 10, Rev. John Elmore, Rev. Fred and Clara Buchanan, and Don and Kathy Beatty completed damage assessments in Bamberg to lay the foundation for an ERT response on January 11.

On January 11, two ERT teams with two ERT trailers and a skid steer responded to the town of Bamberg where an EF2 tornado wreaked havoc through much of downtown.

A large focus was placed on tarping a damaged portion of roof on top of Main Street United Methodist Church, which had gaping holes in the steep roof. This called for the building of a wooden structure to support a tarp and use of a high-ranging bucket truck provided by my son William Robinson, who was in Bamberg working on downed power lines with his company NorthStar Utilities.

"On the majority of our responses into disaster areas we face just that—disastrous and often chaotic situations," Evans said. "This response was no exception. Due to the damage being on one end of the steep roof, we could not assess the roof and had to build a special wooden form to hold the tarp atop the gaping holes in the roof. I had assessed the damage the day before, so Billy Robinson purchased lumber to build the form, but when we started building it, we had to make it even bigger that we expected. This added to the difficulty of the situation

William Robinson works out of his bucket high atop Main Street UMC in Bamberg to help spread out a tarp.

as far as how we would physically be able to get the form on top of the steep roof and then work safely to place a tarp over it and secure it all down.

"Billy's son William owns NorthStar Utilities, and they had been called to the town to work on downed power lines and restoring electrical power. Billy talked to William, and when we had the form ready, William brought one of their high-ranging bucket trucks and helped us accomplish the daunting task. Without the bucket truck the task could not have been completed.

"God always has a plan and way of making things happen and missions successful as long as we have faith and walk steadfast in his lighted path. As Proverbs 3:6 says, 'In all your ways acknowledge him, and he shall direct your paths'" (NKJV).

Volunteers spread throughout Bamberg into three other teams doing chain-saw work on downed trees, removing debris from storm damaged homes and yards, tarping damaged roofs, and witnessing and encouraging survivors in the name of Jesus Christ.

At least six homes and families were helped.

In addition to Evans, ERT responders included Bill Turner, Don and Kathy Beatty, Danny McKowen, Darrel Briggs, Mark Honge, Rev. Cynthia Williams, Sherra Yates, Jayne Schafer, Nancy Goff, Rev. Fred Buchanan, Bud Parker, Dan Dowbridge and Monica Tilley. Other specialized volunteers assisting were South Carolina United Methodist Orangeburg District Superintendent Rev. Ken Nelson, William Robinson with NorthStar Utilities, and Mike Baldwin of Bamberg, who used his skid steer to help.

On January 11, a third team comprising Chuck Marshall, Phil Griswold, Ward Smith, Felix Vazquez, Trudy Robinson, and myself responded with an ERT trailer to the Orangeburg County towns of Santee and Bowman. At each location, we were faced with daunting dangerous situations where fifty- to thirty-foot sections of tin roof had been ripped off mobile homes, exposing their roofs to the weather and rain. Both were unique yet dangerous situations, prompting what came to be a God-sized task.

Our team had to literally cut strips using a Sawzall in the partially attached tin roofs that were laying on the ground and hoist them up by hand and rope back onto the roof truss, all while taking care not to get cut with the very sharp tin or fall through into the home or off the damaged structural members. We then placed duct tape over the sharp edges and completely tarped the homes over the replaced tin roofs. This daunting task took us all day and into the night. At both locations, families were still living out of the severely damaged structures and had all their furniture and possessions inside.

"We had never seen anything like this—two roofs peeled off like a can opener with the far sides still attached and the homes over fourteen miles apart caused by microburst," Smith explained.

Bricks and debris scattered Main Street in Bamberg.

Smith added, "After cutting the tin into ten-foot strips that we could manage, we cut a hole big enough for a rope to go through in the top of each section. Then three of us would pull and work the tin sections up and over the roof, while two members on the ground used a makeshift 'T' they formed out of wood to push up on the tin. We had to walk on small two-by-two-inch rafters, which made the task more difficult. We then placed duct tape over the sharp edges of the tin so it would not cut us or the tarp we placed on top of it after we screwed the tin down.

"Rain was expected the next day, so we drove to Bowman and repeated the same task on another mobile home with the exact same situation. We worked into the dark to complete the task to keep the families dry and safe.

"In both homes, the families had nowhere else to stay and were extremely thankful. We were worn out, but also felt extremely thankful and blessed by God to be used in two of his miraculous blessings."

On Oak Street in Bowman, a man came up to my wife, Trudy, and stated how amazed he was that total strangers from across South Carolina, who had no affiliation with the homeowners, would give of their time, finances, and physical efforts while taking on such a dangerous task to help others in dire need. Many people had passed by to look and take photos, but no one had stopped to help in any way, the man continued.

The man told her, "I want to be a part of a true ministry like yours that goes beyond the church walls and directly into the danger zones to help others in dire need. This is the church in action as I have never seen it before!"

All three teams worked especially hard to get all the disaster work completed on January 11 given pending severe storms and more soaking rain predicted for the next day. We were able to finish all known emergent needs.

Our main focus was to remove fallen trees and debris from the roofs of damaged homes and tarp them to prevent further damage. We thank our Lord and savior Jesus Christ for the honor and privilege of serving in this wonderful, exciting, and extremely fulfilling ministry of care, love, and devotion to helping others in dire need.

—*Billy Robinson*

True Worship in Action

On January 11, 2024, several ERT teams responded to damage from the Janu-

Trudy Robinson talks to homeowner Emma.

ary 9 tornadoes and severe storms. At one in particular, on Oak Street in Bowman where I arrived after the work had begun, I was talking with the homeowner about what it was like when the storm was actually happening. She had her three grandchildren for the night and stated the storm came so fast that she gathered them all together in the safest place she could find. Through the grace of God, none of them even had a scratch. When she was able to actually see the damage the tornado had done to her home, she discovered the top had been peeled back as if a can opener had been used.

As we were talking, a neighbor appeared out of nowhere and tapped the homeowner on her shoulder, saying, "Emma, now this is true worship, outside the walls of the church."

The man continued to say this was an old neighborhood where everyone was close, grew up together, and he had seen everyone riding and walking by to look at and take pictures of her damaged home. But no one, even himself, had stopped to offer her anything from a warm blanket, food, a tarp, or help in any way. He was so amazed that a group of total strangers from all across South Carolina, who didn't know her at all, would give of their time, finances ,and physical efforts, taking on such a dangerous task to help repair her roof at no cost to her.

He concluded his conversation, with tears in his eyes, saying, "Now this is true ministry, beyond the walls of the church, doing what God calls us to do by showing the love of Jesus, the church in action as I have never seen it before. I want to be a part of this!"

The neighbor then just disappeared as quickly as he came.

—*Trudy W. Robinson*

Chapter 56

'Thankful to be Alive'
April 25-26, 2024

On April 20, 2024, the city of Rock Hill, South Carolina, was slammed by a ninety-mile per hour storm that produced a powerful hailstorm, with hail ranging from a quarter in size to as big as baseballs.

The storm and hail devastated the area, toppling many trees and sandblasting the siding of homes, cars, and anything in its path. Many vehicles and homes had their windows broken, and a number of vehicles were totaled.

South Carolina's United Methodist Volunteers in Mission Early Response Team stepped up to help many Rock Hill residents.

Elaine Thomas, of Washington Street, said she was extremely thankful to be alive.

"It was a very terrifying storm as I was caught in it driving," she told us. "The huge hail pounded my car so bad it left one-inch dents all over my car, and then the windows started breaking. Even the windshield started to break in. I got really scared then, but by the loving grace of God, I survived. When I got home, I saw that my big cedar tree in front with three trunks was blocking my wheelchair ramp to my home and the front yard. I am so thankful to the United Methodist volunteers who came to my rescue and cut up the fallen trees. I do not know when or how the fallen trees would have been taken care of if they had not come to the rescue."

On Crawford Street a similar situation occurred. A young couple was on their way home when the powerful storm hit. They pulled into their mother's driveway and rushed into the home amid the strong wind, rain, and hail. They were

Hail devastated the area, toppling trees and sandblasting the siding of homes, cars, and anything in its path. Many vehicles and homes had their windows broken, and a lot of vehicles were totaled.

in the home for only a minute when a giant tree came crashing down, crushing their car and falling onto the roof of the home. Anyone in the car would have been instantly killed. We gave the couple some scripture resources, as we do at every home we visit, and prayed for them. We then put our faith into action and cut the fallen tree off the roof and away from the home, piling the debris into piles that could be picked up by town workers.

It was amazing that no one was killed in this severe a storm. We cut trees and tarped broken windows and roofs for two days, working on six homes. The most important things we do, though, are to help the survivors cope with the disaster and meet their needs as best we can.

We show them the love of Jesus through our actions and our prayers, plus the scripture resources we leave with them that have eternal rewards. We give to them, but God always gives us back such wonderful blessings that you cannot put a price tag on this.

ERT responders were Don and Kathy Beatty, Dan Dowbridge, Rev. Monica Tilley, Danny McKeown, Mike Luther, Kathy Parker, Rev. Mike Evans, Marvin Horton, David Armstrong, Curtis Burnett, Greg Whitlow, Ward Smith, Jim Smith, and me. Special thanks to Cornerstone Methodist Church for hosting and feeding us.

—*Billy Robinson*

Chapter 57

'Onward Christian Soldiers'
July 17, 2024

On July 18, 2024, the South Carolina United Methodist Volunteers in Mission Early Response Team headed to Bamberg, South Carolina, to help our Baptist brothers tarp a severely damaged roof from a January tornado that devastated portions of Bamberg. Back when it happened, our disaster teams responded in force and worked on multiple homes and on Main Street United Methodist Church, which had a severely damaged roof. Six months later, we returned to assist.

Our Baptist counterparts were working on the Pine Street home of Mr. and Mrs. Jonathan Mitchell and their eight grandkids. Mrs. Mitchell is on dialysis with Stage Four kidney disease, and the family has been struggling to make ends meet while taking care of the grandkids also. Because of their financial struggles, they had to let their homeowner's insurance lapse prior to the tornado. The family is very humble and caring, and they tried taking care of the situation themselves, until they realized they could not.

Bamberg First Baptist found out about their need and took action, which started with our combined mission to tarp their leaking roof, which had multiple holes in it from a tree that fell on it during the tornado. Now the original tarps were degrading and tearing apart. The family is attending Bamberg First Baptist, and the church is looking into further ways to help them.

We prayerfully began the mission in a wonderful sense of unity as a Christian community coming together to help and show Jesus's love to this caring and loving family. The church of Jesus Christ came together in one accord as the church should do every day.

It was a hot July day, but the Mitchells offered us cool refreshments and were so grateful even though they were going through such hard times. It was wonderful to see the love of Jesus flowing through them as it was also flowing through all of us back to them.

Responding from First Baptist were Ronnie Smith, Bruce Watson, and Perry Hutto. ERT volunteers were Felix and Misty Vazquez and myself.

God's Holy Spirit was surely in this place and wrapped it in warm loving care, which included us applying a 31- by 50-foot tarp on the roof.

The mission was best summed up by Ligon Hutto of Bamberg First Baptist. Hutto was on his way to another appointment, but as he drove by the Mitchell house, the Holy Spirit came over him with a simple but wonderful message for all of us. He approached us, and as he did, he got so emotional that he could not speak.

Finally, with his voice still cracking and full of emotion, he shouted out he words the Holy Spirit had laid upon him: "Onward, Christian soldiers!"

—*Billy Robinson*

Felix Vazquez nails down a tarp on a damaged home in Bamberg.

Chapter 58

Phenomenal Task, Godly Determination, and Cold Watermelon
August 1, 2024

The early morning hours of July 31, 2024, sent straight line winds through the City of Orangeburg, South Carolina, damaging some downtown businesses and crashing a huge oak tree into a home on Sherwood Drive. No one was injured, but the main portion of this huge oak was on and into the home of Kenneth Fairy. Portions of the trunk were in the home, and several big branches had pierced the roof and reached into the home. The family was desperate for help. They especially wanted the tree cut off as best could be and tarped to prevent further damage from any future rains.

They contacted Orangeburg Emergency Services Director Billy Staley, who called me.

I was in the hospital in Lexington recovering from two serious intestinal bleeds and was extremely weak. But by the grace of God, I was able to call on several people with the South Carolina United Methodist Volunteers in Mission Early Response Team and got Felix and Misty Vazquez to meet Staley and assess the situation. I also put out texts to several of our team leaders. When Felix and Misty replied that it was a complicated but doable job, the team leaders sprang into action, coordinating a next-day response.

On August 1, 2024, a faithful and determined team of six responded with one ERT trailer and started work early on a day that had a predicted 110-degree heat index. The tasks were phenomenal for the small team, but with help from the homeowner and a family member, they had the hot, humid, hard, and difficult

Straight line winds caused a huge oak tree to crash into a home on Sherwood Drive.

job complete eight hours later. This included mustering up the energy and pure God-given determination to climb onto the hot roof after all team members had experienced some form of heat exhaustion and tarp the roof, preventing an upcoming rain from causing further damage.

Watermelon and mandated cooldown sessions helped them complete the task, plus the love, will, and desire to help others in need just as Jesus helps and loves us.

Team members were Rev. Mike Evans, Don and Kathy Beatty, Danny McKeown, and Felix and Misty Vazquez.

—Billy Robinson

Chapter 59

Brothers and Sisters in Jesus Christ
August 6-22, 2024

Tropical Storm Debby hit South Carolina with four small tornadoes, and several places saw straight line wind damage on August 6, 2024. Flooding rains continued for at least a week after in portions of the Lowcountry.

In the first days, several areas across the state were helped by the South Carolina United Methodist Volunteers in Mission Early Response Team with limb removal.

On August 14, my wife, Trudy, and I took four ERT fans and three personal ones to Canaan United Methodist Church in Ridgeville in care of Rev. James Smith to be used in flooded areas of the Family Life Center and possibly the sanctuary. Their church had major damage in the 2015 floods, and ERT teams helped muck out and clean out the church for weeks. This time, it only flooded the floors and a stage area, where they cut holes in just above floor level to place fans so it would dry out.

Canaan's cemetery had significant flooding with water still standing in it. Two caskets had popped up out of the ground. One had been put back into place, but the other had to be secured and put back after the cemetery dried out.

On August 15, an ERT team of six—myself plus Jerry Harris, Rev. Melissa Williams, Frank Gramling, Felix Vazquez, and Rev. Sheera Yates—responded with ERT Trailer SC-08 to cut limbs off a home and place a 10- by 22-foot tarp on a roof in Bowman at the home of Sharon Neals. A large dead tree had fallen onto the roof of the home, creating a big hole that water poured into. Family had placed a four-by-eight-foot sheet of plyboard over it, but it only slowed the rains down. Water still continued to pour in. Other tree limbs were on the home that we also had to cut away. This exposed two other small holes in another portion of the roof that we were able to repair by using tar and working some new shingles into.

We then headed to the home of Nancy Perry on Chestnut Avenue in Denmark, after stopping by Wee Bakery in Denmark for a fine meal. We work very hard on these missions, but we also take the opportunity to enjoy a good meal

Rev. Melissa Williams holds the ladder so Jerry Harris can safely nail down a tarp on a Bowman home.

together every time we get the chance. We cut a pile of limbs off two sheds, one of which was being used as a business, being careful to stay out of an area that had flooded with contaminated water.

On August 16, Jerry Harris put in a day's work repairing a damaged roof on Highway 61 in Ridgeville. He worked on twenty-eight nail pops and tack heads using tar plus replacement shingles in various locations. The home also had much flooding and water damage, and there may be further cleanup needed depending on the homeowner.

On August 22, another team of six—myself plus Harris, Williams, Vazquez, and Don and Kathy Beatty—responded with ERT Trailer SC-08 to a home on Race Track Road near Elloree. This was a deferred maintenance home whose roof was in terrible shape with many bad boards and spots and multiple leaks. Most of the fascia boards were rotten. We tarped the entire home using a 63- by 33-foot tarp after we cut several limbs away from the roof. The elderly woman living there had no means of repairing the home.

We get called to a lot of deferred maintenance homes that leak and such. Our mission is disaster response, but we help with these types of homes in special situations where there is no other immediate means of help. We do not have the

Jerry Harris cuts limbs off a home in Bowman while Felix Vazquez assists removing limbs.

number of volunteers or finances to place tarps on homes simply needing a new roof. We often refer people in need to local churches or other organizations that may be able to assist them.

We have been blessed with so many wonderful, kind, generous, compassionate, gifted, and loving volunteers over the past twenty years. They constantly give of their time, energy, finances, and selves to help complete strangers in need—usually in dire need.

It has been one of the biggest honors and privileges of my life to know them, work hard with, minister with, cry with, sweat and bleed with, cut up with, tease with, have fun with, and refer to them as brothers and sisters in the name of Jesus Christ.

—Billy Robinson

Chapter 60

Mega Storm, Mega Damage, Mega Help
September 27-October 13, 2024

The Category 4 Hurricane Helene came ashore in the Big Bend area of Florida on September 26, 2024, bringing with it destruction throughout Florida, Georgia, South Carolina, North Carolina, Tennessee and Virginia. The storm killed more than 230 people. Florida saw wind and flooding, Western North Carolina saw unprecedented flooding that left more than 120 dead, and Georgia and South Carolina saw massive tree damage.

Much of the focus has been on North Carolina's flooding, but South Carolina had a massive amount of damage from wind and tornados, with many portions of the state looking like a bomb went off. The hurricane toppled trees in the thousands if not more, from the mid portion of the state to the North Carolina and Georgia borders. Many of these trees crashed onto and into homes, blocked roadways, and tore down countless miles of power lines, leaving some communities without power for two weeks.

Around 4:00 a.m. September 27, South Carolina started getting hit with flooding bands and tropical- to hurricane-force winds, including tornadoes. Power went out en masse.

At 6:00 a.m., I received a call from Ann Fairey, a member of North United Methodist Church, North, who has a lot of health problems requiring her to be on constant oxygen. She stated her power had gone off and she was out of oxygen and in desperate need of some. She knew I was a paramedic and volunteered with my local fire department. I and my wife, Trudy, pressed through the darkness, pouring rain, tropical force winds, and falling limbs to obtained two oxygen cylinders from our department and a generator from my shed. On the way to her, we had to dodge falling trees and low powerlines because of broken power poles

The ERT team gathers onsite in Lincolnton, Georgia.

and trees on lines. A power company stopped us at one point, saying the roads were hazardous. We got to her just in time to get her oxygen back on and prevent her from going into respiratory distress.

As we left, we responded with North Volunteer Fire Department to two vehicle wrecks. It was still dark and hazardous when we arrived at the first one, where a man had run into a very big fallen pine tree. He was okay and the scene secured, though trees were literally falling all around us. We got him away from other trees and proceeded to the second wreck. That one involved a tractor trailer that had been driving through a low-lying area on Salley Road near the North Edisto River when two big trees fell in front of him. The driver hit the brakes, but the trees fell right in front of him, so he hit both hard. The crash tore parts of the cab off, then veered him off the road into a river landing access road, then head-on into a big pine tree. He was shaken up but said he planned to stay with his truck and trailer, which was carrying parts for Boeing.

Trees continued to fall as we left him to cut emergency egress roads out. An hour later, three pine trees crashed onto his rig, and one big tree penetrated into the rig's trailer section. By the grace of God, the driver was not injured throughout the entire storm.

Scenes such as this was played out across the path of Helene as first responders risked their lives to save others. Two volunteer firefighters with Circle Volunteer Fire Department, Chad Satcher and Landon Bodie, were killed in Saluda

Felix Vazquez uses a 36-inch Stihl chainsaw to cut a hug red oak out of a driveway near North after Hurricane Helene.

County responding to a structure fire when a tree fell on their fire truck. One other firefighter was killed in Georgia as he was helping cut out roadways and a falling tree hit the cab of his fire truck.

Eight inches of rain that first day brought floodwaters up to the threshold of my home in North, with five more inches to come. By the grace of God, we had a total of seven generators—between South Carolina's UMVIM Early Response Team, North VFD, and personal ones—that we handed out on the first day and into that night, with four going to people on oxygen. We also provided them with fuel as needed, which soon became a scarce item.

Thousands of trees were cut out of main roadways throughout the path of Helene on September 27 and 28 thanks to ERT efforts with help from the Department of Transportation, the Global Methodist Church's Disaster Response Team, and many volunteer and paid fire departments across the path of the storm. We started at daybreak in South Carolina and continued for two days. Next the focus shifted to side roads and access to people's homes. Then came the removing of trees from on and in homes, plus tarping the damaged holes in roofs and windows. Many people had trees in their yards and other storm damage.

Helene was a mega storm that caused mega damage that required mega help. This destructive storm tore families and entire communities apart but also brought out the best in people and responders. As in all disasters, we respond better and more proficiently when we respond together in one accord with one goal in mind: "Christian love in action" to quickly and proficiently meet the dire needs of the storm survivors. We did just that as we responded side by side with Baptists, Global Methodists, Mennonites, Samaritan's Purse, Team Rubicon, and others. In a coordinated effort, we were able to help hundreds of people by cutting out access to their homes, tarping their roofs, providing them with basic needs, and spiritually ministering to them in loving and caring ways with prayer and scripture items.

South Carolina UMVIM ERT members responded in most hard-hit areas of the state, such as parts of Orangeburg County, Manning, Edgefield, Johnston, Spartanburg, Pelzer, Chesney, Lyman, Duncan, Easley, Anderson, Clover, Lake Wylie, North Augusta, and Aiken, as well as into Lincolnton, Georgia. In at least seven cases, we cut trees off our own homes or those of family members. We were able to show the love and care of Jesus in all situations.

Some cases stand out, such as a lady we could not help just outside of Edgefield, whose two-story home had its second floor crushed by a huge oak tree that had been removed using a big excavator. The remaining brick outer wall was leaning and about to fall. What remained of the second floor was unstable, and there was no way to tarp the damaged area to prevent further damage. Her husband had recently died, and she had family coming in the next day to help her salvage items. Her faith remained strong, and she continuously thanked us even though we did nothing physical for her. What we did was hold hands in a circle and pray for her and hug her to let her know we care—but most importantly, that Jesus cares and loves her.

We often witness families coming to the aid of their family members. One of our members, Kevin Douglass, lives in Cross, and he called me in desperation the morning the storm hit as he and his neighbor both had trees on their home with roof damage. We were still in emergency mode and not able to get to him for days. After a pleading call to Rev. Ken Phelps, Ken and others came to the rescue of Kevin and his neighbor, removing the trees and tarping the roofs as needed.

We experienced fathers pleading with us to help their children in need and children asking us to help their parents. It was a hard and trying time but also a joyful time as we witnessed such awesome love and caring.

We used the Fred Device often in this response. The Fred Device is a heavy metal A-frame invented by Rev. Fred Buchanan. Teams used it often to relieve tension from a fallen tree on a home so we can safely cut a tree off and away from a home.

Supplies are always critical to our ministry, thus we prepare ahead of time with chainsaws, extra chains, fuel oil, tarps, slats for tarps, etc. In this case, we ran low on slats and some other essentials in various areas, but God always came through in the nick of time. In one instance, Terry Rawls drove across the state to deliver slats to us that he'd made on his farm.

There will surely continue to be storms in our lives, whether natural disasters or various other kinds, such as health or financial disasters. One thing is always certain and never changes with the winds of time: God's awesome love for us. It

Above, Danny McKeown, Felix Vazquez, Rev. Mike Evans, and Don Beatty assess a severely damaged two-story home near Edgefield. Below, Rudy Dinkins cuts a tree off his daughter's home in North Augusta as Billy Robinson keeps the cut log from damaging the roof.

is an honor and privilege for us to be used as his hands and feet to people in need.

Sometimes it seems harder to get people willing to volunteer, but we will continue to carry the cross of disaster response, for Jesus is our commander and we are joyfully his servants.

—Billy Robinson

Chapter 61

The Importance of Strong ERT Training

Training has been one of our most essential components to having volunteers fully equipped for the dangerous tasks we face on every response.

We have strived to equip all our South Carolina United Methodist Volunteers in Mission Early Response Team volunteers with proper protective equipment, safety gear, tools, devices, finances, and resources, including trailers and machinery. We have strived just as hard to train our volunteers to equip their minds with the knowledge and godly wisdom needed to accomplish the sometimes-daunting task presented to us on our disaster responses.

This has required a variety of training props and aids to emphasis the importance of such things as safety with chainsaws, tarping a roof, mucking/cleaning out, assessing, etc.

Spiritual matters are of extreme importance as well, so a lot of emphasis is also placed on how we approach and relay Christian love to the survivors of disasters, other faith-based volunteers, emergency workers, coordinators, and anyone else we might encounter. Then there is the critical matter of ministering to our volunteers and making sure they are equipped with the knowledge of critical incident stress and managing feelings of overwhelm and stress.

The nature of our ministry requires a lot of dangerous work, so basic first aid training for all is strongly encouraged. All ERT teams comprise at least one person specially trained in first aid and well equipped to perform any aid required, which often is used for those we come to serve as well.

Our trainers and instructors are special people with the desire and drive to go above and beyond what is required to a higher level of knowledge. They are car-

Above, instructors demonstrate how to properly tarp a roof. Below left, an instructor leads a session during a Fort Mill ERT class. Below right, as of this writing, ERT has 19 UMCOR-certified trainers.

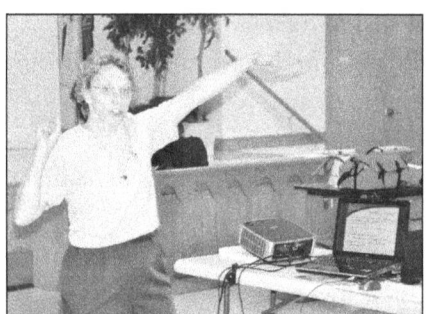

ing and loving people who God has given the special abilities to teach the skill levels needed for disaster response.

The United Methodist Committee on Relief sets forth a rigid training curriculum that it required for all its UMCOR trained instructors. This requires passing a special in-person training course that UMCOR staff offer at special request. Then an UMCOR evaluator actually comes to a training class and evaluates each instructor to make sure they have what it takes to do the job.

Over the past twenty years, we have been truly blessed with some wonderful, God-sent trainers and instructors, including 19 UMCOR-certified instructors and many other trainers and people who help with set up, props, and more.

Our UMCOR-certified instructors have included Nathan Welch of Simpson-

Above, Danny Thompson leads a session. Below, Billy Robinson and his helpers show trainees how to tarp around a chimney.

ville, Mark and Betty Springer of Anderson, Rev. Fred Buchanan, Revs. Don and Karen Upson, Rev. Bob Alan, Dan Dowbridge and Rev. Monica Tilley of Clover, Rev. William "Buddy" Phillips of Murrells Inlet, Caroline Dennis of Greenville, Rev. Mike Evans of Edgefield, Kathy Beatty of Lexington, Ward Smith of Columbia, Rev. Amanda Richardson of Greenville, Rev. Stephen Turner of Anderson, Rev. John Elmore of Holly Hill, Trudy Robinson of North, and myself.

Backing us up as trainers in specialized fields have been Chuck Marshall of Chesnee, Felix and Misty Vazquez of North, Danny Thompson of Anderson, Miles Knight of Irmo, Troy and Renee Thomas of Summerville, Casey Canonge of Summerville, Terry Rawls of Pomaria, and Rev. Ken Phelps of Manning.

—*Billy Robinson*

An instructor reviews a point during an ERT class in Boiling Springs.

Above, instructors show a class how to safely use a ladder during an ERT training in Summerville. Below, chainsaws are always a fun part of the lesson.

Conclusion

ERT from the Inside Out

The past twenty years of being a part of the South Carolina United Methodist Volunteers in Mission Early Response Team has been a blessing from God.

But for the past twelve years I have experienced ERT from the inside out, watching firsthand from our home more responses than we have been able to count—into the high hundreds, probably close to 1,000 or even more.

Being married to Billy Robinson, South Carolina ERT coordinator, for the past twelve years is a blessing in itself. But to see how the ERT response is carried out step by step, and how it has been a blessing to so many over the years, has been exciting, interesting, rewarding, heartwarming, heartbreaking at times, and (sometimes!) even tiring, to say the least.

After we were married just a short time, around 2:00 one morning, Billy received a fire call from Orangeburg County Emergency Services Dispatch, where he has been a volunteer with North Volunteer Fire Department for forty years. I made the statement, "Do you have to go?"

His response to me—with his hands held out in front of him, palms up, stern-faced to try to make me understand—was, "This is what I do."

This is what I call my most rewarding "a-ha moment" in regard to all of his ERT work and responses with North Fire Department, his paid job at Savannah River Site Fire Department, or anything to do with helping repair someone's life through ERT or saving lives or belongings on medical or fire calls.

My "a-ha moment" then led me to the saying, "If you can't beat them, join them." So as I was already a member of ERT, I joined the North Fire Department also!

Having said all of this, God has blessed all of us with the strength and protection for the tasks set before Billy and all the leaders and volunteers.

To sum up all the years of responses in a short form is impossible, but in trying to give a summary, I would say on each individual response, from the moment the weather stations start reporting that a named hurricane has been spotted in the Gulf or a weather system of any type has formed, the Robinson household becomes somewhat of an Emergency Response Center of its own. This looks like:

- A continued watching of television and phone weather reports;
- Many district disaster coordinators planning sessions via phone calls, emails, text, etc.;
- Calls from out-of-state teams offering their availability to help (where so many friends/relationships have developed over these twenty years);
- Calls from South Carolina volunteers eager to know when they can respond;
- Late-night planning and emails to alert volunteers of any possible responses (1:30 or 2:00 a.m. was not unusual for Billy, and then he would have to report for work at the Savannah River Site at 7:00 a.m., where he was a captain/paramedic);
- Calls from so many other organizations planning to combine their response efforts; and
- Watching the organized response structure of being invited to respond if it's out of our response area.

The responses where no invitation is necessary, such as in our state or local areas, are somewhat quicker and mount up to many, many more but also require hours and days of preparation. This includes daily and late-night emails; notification of district coordinators and trained volunteers; building of individual teams; and coordinating where/what time to respond. It has been like watching a well-oiled machine at work.

When at last the trailers with "Christian Love in Action" pull out of the yard filled with many dedicated volunteers, whether I'm on the response or watching from our front door, it's such a rewarding, heartwarming moment. In these many moments, along with the response itself, words aren't enough to describe how it feels being the "hands and feet" of God and getting the honor of showing God's love for all of his people.

There has and I'm sure will continue to be a God-inspired unconditional eagerness that has been so inspiring to me, and I am so thankful to have been a part of this for twenty years. Billy and I use the saying around our home that we

From his living room, Billy Robinson coordinates late-night planning and emails to keep volunteers in the loop about how they can help.

have the privilege of working with the "best of the best" of God's people on these responses.

There have been times when, as a wife out of concern for her husband, I've had to plead with Billy to get some rest. But I should also say that was to no avail.

I want to make it clear that even though being Billy's wife I'm "a little" prejudiced—and I know there are so many other volunteers and leaders' spouses feeling the same way—I can only see and tell the story of what's happening in our home where most information eventually ends up. Only through the involved planning and preparation of God's blessings of so many leaders and trained volunteers are these responses possible. To God be the glory!

I think I would be derelict in telling my story not to mention all the planning that has to be done during the years to make these responses possible, through countless trainings over the state by the team trainers, who I would like to add had to attend a three-day course sponsored by the United Methodist Committee on Relief and then be evaluated and approved by a "tough" UMCOR employee even to become a trainer. Billy was the first one to be trained in South Carolina.

In addition to all of this, there have to be materials to work with and trailers to work from, all of which cost a considerable amount of money. And there again, God has blessed us through hard work in raising monies and donations from those who have received help from an ERT response over the years. For every dollar raised and all the dedicated work of many, to God be the glory.

I would also like to remember several of the individuals who were very instrumental in beginning South Carolina UMVIM ERT— to name just a few, Dr. Mike and Mary Carolyn Watson, Rev. George Strait, and Rev. Nick and Judy Elliott. These individuals, as well as many, many others, would at just the right time (especially when things were stressful around the house during a response!) make a phone call or send an email to Billy, along with many cards from Mrs. Mary Carolyn Watson, which would lift our spirits and spur him on to completion of the response.

There are two quotes we use often in our home that I feel sum up why we must continue to be God's hands and feet here on earth.

The first is by the Christian missionary Elisabeth Elliot: "I'm convinced that there are a good many things in this life that we really can't do anything about but that God wants us to do something with." And the second is by her husband, Jim Elliot: "He is no fool who gives what he cannot keep to gain what he cannot lose."

To God be the glory for twenty years of the honor and privilege of being a small part of being God's hands and feet here on this earth.

—*Trudy W. Robinson*

Billy and Trudy Robinson, ready for mission.

South Carolina UMVIM ERT Favorite Mission Scriptures

Psalm 145:3: "Great is the Lord and most worthy of praise. His greatness no one can fathom."

Psalm 107:1: "Give thanks to the Lord, for he is good; his love endures forever."

John 3:16: "For God so loved the world that he gave his one and only Son, that whoever believes in him shall not perish but have eternal life."

Philippians 4:13: "I can do all this through him who gives me strength."

Isaiah 40:31: "But those who hope in the Lord will renew their strength. They will soar on wings like ea-gles; they will run and not grow weary, they will walk and not be faint."

John 8:12: "I am the light of the world. Whoever follows me will never walk in darkness, but will have the light of life."

Joshua 24:15: "But as for me and my household, we will serve the Lord."

Ephesians 6:14-17: "Stand firm then, with the belt of truth buckled around your waist, with the breast-plate of righteousness in place, and with your feet fitted with the readiness that comes from the gospel of peace. In addition to all this, take up the shield of faith, with which you can extinguish all the flaming arrows of the evil one. Take the helmet of salvation and the sword of the Spirit, which is the word of God."

Joshua 1:9: "Do not be afraid; do not be discouraged, for the Lord your God will be with you wherever you go."

John 15:13: "Greater love has no one than this: to lay down one's life for one's friends."

Proverbs 3:5-6: "Trust in the Lord with all your heart and lean not on your own understanding; in all your ways submit to him, and he will make your paths straight."

1 Corinthians 16:13: "Be on your guard; stand firm in the faith; be courageous; be strong."

Psalm 46:1: "God is our refuge and strength, an ever-present help in trouble."

Psalm 29:11: "The Lord gives strength to his people; the Lord blesses his people with peace."

Hebrews 11:1: "Now faith is confidence in what we hope for and assurance about what we do not see."

Psalm 23: "The Lord is my shepherd, I lack nothing. He makes me lie down in green pastures, he leads me beside quiet waters, he refreshes my soul. He guides me along the right paths for his name's sake. Even though I walk through the darkest valley, I will fear no evil, for you are with me; your rod and your staff, they comfort me. You prepare a table before me in the presence of my enemies. You anoint my head with oil; my cup overflows. Surely your goodness and love will follow me all the days of my life, and I will dwell in the house of the Lord forever."

Psalm 27:1: "The Lord is my light and my salvation— whom shall I fear? The Lord is the stronghold of my life— of whom shall I be afraid?"

Matthew 17:20: "If you have faith as small as a mustard seed, you can say to this mountain, 'Move from here to there,' and it will move. Nothing will be impossible for you.'"

Isaiah 43:2: "When you walk through the fire, you will not be burned; the flames will not set you ablaze."

1 Corinthians 13: The entirety of the love chapter.

For more information on how to support the South Carolina UMVIM Early Response Team, visit https://www.umcsc.org/disaster-response

www.ingramcontent.com/pod-product-compliance
Lightning Source LLC
Chambersburg PA
CBHW050858160426
43194CB00011B/2200

WHAT PEOPLE ARE SAYING ABOUT
THE FASTING COMPANION

I challenge you to immerse yourself in the profound journey offered by *The Fasting Companion*, where spiritual wisdom meets scientific insight to unlock the transformative power of fasting. Dr. Thando Sibanda weaves daily scripture-based themes with prayer prompts and reflections, creating a holistic guide to navigate the emotional, physical, and spiritual challenges of a 21-day fast. This invaluable resource is a must-read for anyone eager to deepen their spiritual life and experience fasting's full potential.

—Bishop Tony Dunn, D.Min.
NewDay Global Network

The Fasting Companion by Dr. Thando Sibanda is an invaluable resource for anyone seeking transformative spiritual, physical, and emotional renewal. With the wisdom of a seasoned spiritual leader, teacher, and scholar, Dr. Sibanda skillfully connects Scripture with scientific insights, offering a holistic and accessible approach to fasting that is both practical and deeply impactful. This book is essential for anyone ready to experience the fullness of God's transformative power, through fasting, and unlock new levels of renewal and growth in every area of life.

—Dr David Molapo
President: ICAN Leadership Institute Africa

The Fasting Companion isn't just a guide—it's your breakthrough blueprint, igniting transformation and unlocking the power of fasting to renew your spirit, body, and mind!

—Dr Sean Sibanda
Author/Speaker/Consultant